# When South Carolina Was an Armed Camp

## The Reconstruction Essays of Belton O'Neall Townsend

Edited by John Hammond Moore

HOME
HOUSE
PRESS
CHARLESTON

## Advance Praise for *When South Carolina Was an Armed Camp*

Reading the Reconstruction essays of Belton O'Neall Townsend is a revelation. Of course Townsend shared many of the same racial attitudes that dominated white Southerners, but he had a rare ability to step back and speak truthfully about the shortcomings of his fellow white South Carolinians. It is that combination of incisive and vivid prose and remarkable candor that gives us a rare first-hand insight into social and political conditions in South Carolina during this tumultuous period.

—Dan Carter, author of *When the War Was Over: The Failure of Self-Reconstruction in the South, 1865-1867; Scottsboro: A Tragedy of the American South; The Politics of Rage: George Wallace, the Origins of the New Conservatism, and the Transformation of American Politics;* and *From George Wallace to Newt Gingrich: Race in the Conservative Counterrevolution, 1963-1994*

This book is a unique and exceptionally revealing window into South Carolina's troubled Reconstruction history. Edited with a poignant introduction by John Hammond Moore, this volume introduces an unconventional view of Reconstruction from a brilliant and unconventional young South Carolinian. A frustrated poet, Belton O'Neall Townsend found fame as a trenchant and brutally honest commentator on Reconstruction South Carolina's politics, society, and morals.

—Lawrence S. Rowland, Distinguished Professor Emeritus, University of South Carolina-Beaufort

The Reconstruction essays of Belton O'Neall Townsend provide a powerful and compelling examination of South Carolina's turbulent history in the decade following the Civil War. The author, a white Carolinian unaffiliated with the Republican Party, shows how the state remained mired in martial conflict, as the contest to control the state was fought with all the relentlessness of a life-and-death struggle.

—Bernard Powers, author of *Black Charlestonians: A Social History, 1822-1885*

# When South Carolina Was an Armed Camp

Published by Home House Press
109 Broad Street
Charleston, South Carolina 29401
www.homehousepress.org

Designed by Paul F. Rossmann
Printed and bound by McNaughton & Gunn,
    Saline, Michigan

First printing

ISBN 978-0-9845580-6-3

COVER ILLUSTRATIONS:
"Worse than Slavery," by Thomas Nast, *Harper's Weekly*, October 24, 1874. Courtesy of the Rubenstein Rare Book and Manuscript Library, Duke University.

Photo of Belton O'Neall Townsend, courtesy of Benjamin T. Zeigler.

## Other books by John Hammond Moore

*Santee Cooper 75 Powering Generations* (2010, with Walter Edgar)

*Carnival of Blood: Dueling, Lynching, and Murder in South Carolina, 1880-1920* (2006)

*Wacko War: Strange Tales from America, 1941-1945* (2001)

*The Winyah Indigo Society of Georgetown, South Carolina, 1755-1998* (1998)

*Southern Homefront, 1861-1865* (1998)

*The Confederate Housewife: Receipts & Remedies, Together with Sundry Suggestions for Garden, Farm & Plantation* (1997)

*The Baileys of Clinton: A South Carolina Family, 1860-1996: The Ancestors & Descendants of Mercer Silas Bailey & Rosanna Lydia Abrams Bailey* (1996)

*Columbia and Richland County: A South Carolina Community, 1740-1990* (1993)

*South Carolina Newspapers* (1988)

*The South Carolina Highway Department, 1917-1987* (1987)

*Wiley: One Hundred and Seventy-Five Years of Publishing* (1981)

*Over-Sexed, Over-Paid & Over Here: Americans in Australia, 1941-1945* (1981)

*The Faustball Tunnel: German POWs in America and Their Great Escape* (1978)

*Australians in America, 1876-1976* (1977)

*Albemarle: Jefferson's County, 1727-1976* (1976)

*The Young Errol: Flynn before Hollywood* (Australia, 1975; U.S. revised ed., 2011)

*The American Alliance: Australia, New Zealand, and the United States, 1940-1970* (1970)

*Research Materials in South Carolina: A Guide* (1967)

## Books Edited by John Hammond Moore

*The Voice of Small-Town America: The Selected Writings of Robert Quillen, 1920-1948* (2008)

*A Plantation Mistress on the Eve of the Civil War: The Diary of Keziah Goodwyn Hopkins Brevard, 1860-1861* (1993)

*South Carolina in the 1880s: A Gazetteer* (1989)

*The Juhl Letters to the Charleston Courier: A View of the South, 1865-1871* (1974)

*Before and After; or, The Relations of the Races at the South* (1967)

# Contents

# Introduction

*By John Hammond Moore*

IN THE LATE 1870S several articles in national publications presented an inside but highly critical view of South Carolina's Reconstruction political and cultural scene. They were shocking to many because they were so frank, and they have been quoted frequently by historians because the unnamed author dared say publicly what others only whispered. For instance, in April 1877 the author explained in the *Atlantic Monthly*,

> There used to prevail in the South an inquisitorial, relentless determination to suppress the truth about the maltreatment of the slaves. Atrocities were frequently perpetrated, yet it was persistently asserted that the negroes were uniformly well treated, were contented and happy, and that all reports to the contrary were malicious lies invented by interested politicians or crazy fanatics. While there are few Southerners who could not have written an abler vindication of Uncle Tom's Cabin than its authoress, on every hand she was denounced as a busybody, a mischief-maker, a fanatic, a lunatic, a liar of the first magnitude; and yet I have heard Southerners, who in formal argument would deny the possibility of any and every event in her matchless exposé, in moments of jovial conversation relate with great gusto anecdotes of how in the good old times they used to hunt down runaway negroes with hounds and guns, brand them, beat them till senseless, and while patrolling at night flog negroes who had passes, "just to hear them beg and hollo." "But all that's gone now," they remark with a sigh, on concluding.[1]

Had any Northerner written this he would have been condemned in every southern drawing room from Richmond to New Orleans. But the author was a young South Carolinian, a native of the Pee Dee town of Florence, and a graduate of the state's leading college. He published six articles starting in 1876, when South Carolina was a battlefield, "an armed camp," as he described the state. At that time, whites ran a terrorist campaign to wrench power away from Northerners, a few South Carolina whites, and most of the native black citizens, some their former slaves, who made up the majority of the population. And he wrote those words, and many more, not in small-circulation journals but in the *New York Tribune* and the *Atlantic Monthly*, two of the North's leading publications. Not surprisingly, the author chose to publish the articles anonymously. They were signed "A South Carolinian," but in 1888 he allowed himself to be identified. He was Belton O'Neall Townsend.

Ironies abound in Townsend's short life. Extremely able, perhaps near genius, this young South Carolinian was a superb scholar, wrote lines in the 1870s that briefly captured national attention, became a respected lawyer and community leader in an emerging rail center, and orchestrated the campaign that made Florence the capital of a new county. While still in his twenties, Townsend headed up two building-and-loan associations, served as worthy master of a local

*Belton O'Neall Townsend. Photo courtesy of Benjamin T. Zeigler.*

Masonic lodge, presided over the activities of a volunteer steam-engine fire company, and helped found a public library and reading room. At age thirty, he courted a young lady of good lineage, married, and subsequently fathered three children. Yet one goal eluded him, the one he craved above all others: to be recognized and praised as a poet. His grandson Eugene N. ("Nick") Zeigler, a distinguished attorney in the community Belton O'Neall Townsend did much to create, conceded the sadness: "So much innate ability and this wild unfulfilled desire to be known as a great poet!"[2]

Even this young man's name is ironic. He was christened in honor of his father's life-long friend, South Carolina Chief Justice John Belton O'Neall, a stalwart temperance leader, whose views were heartily endorsed by the elder Townsend. Yet the son, as both youth and adult, imbibed freely, frequently to excess. In fact, if one can believe random accounts, at the moment the state legislature was creating Florence County in 1888, Townsend was stretched out in a Columbia hotel room, too drunk to savor his triumph. And it is quite

*Benjamin D. Townsend and Mary Brow Townsend, father and mother of Belton O'Neall Townsend. Photos courtesy of Benjamin T. Zeigler.*

possible that liquor played a role in his premature death three years later.[3]

When Townsend's long-anticipated book of poems appeared in 1884, his neighbor George McD. Stoll composed a lengthy "biographical introduction" brimming with praise that, nonetheless, contains this cautionary note:

> Mr. Townsend's chief characteristic may be best put as intense emotionality, which, however, he is able generally either to absolutely smother or turn into rational energy and persistency of action and purpose, through self-discipline and intellectual training. At times, however, it breaks through and makes him do and say very foolish (and to the public unaccountable) things.[4]

Belton O'Neall Townsend was born in Bennettsville, South Carolina, on January 5, 1855, the son of Benjamin D. and Mary Brow Townsend. His father (1815-85), variously described as a merchant, farmer, and bank agent, in 1860 owned thirteen slaves ranging in ages from two to fifty-three and real estate valued at $5,000. His mother (1819-96), a Charleston girl, was the daughter of Captain Thomas Brow; in 1850 her mother, Harriett Brow, probably a widow, was a member of the Bennettsville household.[5]

In addition to Belton there were three other children—Pemalia, who apparently died as an infant in the early 1850s, Constantia (1851-1921), and another son named Cary, two years younger than Belton. Their father, a major in the home guard who probably opposed secession, served briefly as president of the Bank of Georgetown in the early 1860s. Following the war, the family moved from Bennettsville to Society Hill, where he continued to farm. In 1866 he became head of a railroad project, the Cheraw & Darlington, designed to connect Cheraw with various points in North Carolina; ultimately it became part of the Atlantic Coast Line. The chief importance of this enterprise was its link-up with the North Eastern Rail Road, which determined the location of the present city of Florence.

## SOUTH CAROLINA COLLEGE

Belton, who was small of stature, slim, and always looked younger than his years, was an avid reader. As a student, he excelled in composition and demonstrated keen interest in history and chemistry. In 1869, a few months after his fourteenth birthday, he graduated from Society Hill's historic St. David's Academy, but because of academic regulations concerning age, he was unable to enter the South Carolina College (today the University of South Carolina) until October 1870. Townsend was one of about fifty young men to enroll during that session.

In his first year, he completed courses in chemistry; in the second, history and rhetoric; and in the third, mathematics and Greek. Along the way Townsend received special praise ("distinguished") for his accomplishments in rhetoric, history, natural philosophy, and ancient languages, although he struggled with mathematics. The only individual to receive a bachelor of arts degree in 1873 and one of four speakers on Public Day, he delivered an essay on "The Drama." Belton O'Neall Townsend was then eighteen years old.[6]

During these ceremonies, five other students were awarded law degrees, two more completed medical training, and honorary degrees were conferred upon five prominent citizens, among them ex-Attorney General Daniel H. Chamberlain, who soon would become governor. Within a few years, this chance meeting of Townsend and Chamberlain, both on the same platform, would assume special significance.[7]

Copies of this young man's class notes, now at the South Caroliniana Library, together with other personal papers reveal a rigid classroom atmosphere, lectures often closing with a professor signing off, "Respectfully, your obedient servant." Thirty-two pages of comments on the feudal system by the Hon. Robert W. Barnwell, LLD, close with this observation: "The great evil of the feudal system was that it encouraged individuality at the expense of sociability. Our next lesson, young gentlemen, will be Guizot—half of the lesson where we left off. The bell has rung, so good morning." On the other hand, Townsend seems to have taken less seriously Maximilian LaBorde's course in rhetoric, and perhaps with good reason, since this professor said ten meetings and nine lectures would be spent in "nice, old-time conversation." Townsend's notes for the final, pre-exam session open with LaBorde observing he had no doubt they "would get through" and then drift off into ten lines of "&c., &c., &c." repeated over one hundred times, ending with "ad finitum."[8]

But college was not all classwork and note taking. In a letter to his mother, written on November 4, 1870, about a month after arriving in Columbia, he reported, "I am gradually becoming familiarized with my surroundings & the novelty of college life is fast wearing away & as my freshing period is gone I am being admitted more & more to the secrets of the students, & am on the whole well satisfied." His roommate was Frank Beard of Columbia, who graduated in history in 1871 and then studied law before launching a newspaper career. A "waiting boy" named Ben "blacked" their shoes, made up beds, swept the room, ran errands, and did "every thing" they wanted him to do; they were also served by a washerwoman named Betsey. Townsend conceded he did not know their last names. Stressing he had only $10.00 left after paying for their services, young Belton boasted a bit: "My new suit fits splendidly & none of the boys (students) recognize me when I put it on & I venture to say that if I came to the front door at home, & knocked that I would be invited into the parlor & my name asked!" He then uttered a common student plea: "I need another suit <u>badly</u>. <u>All</u> of the students have <u>three</u> suits, & some have <u>six</u>. I have to wear the suit I left home in except on Sundays & it (the suit) is getting sadly out of order. Do try & get me a new suit, & at least another <u>long</u> tail coat if you cannot get the rest."[9]

Ever the dutiful son, Townsend closed with regards to all, adding, "I am wonderfully reconciled to kerosene oil & burn it as fearlessly as you do candles. . . . I am very careful," and a few words concerning campus pranks:

> The students are going on worse this session than at any time since the war. Great bomb shells are let off at night & on Thursday morning the professors got up & upon looking out of doors found all of their gates (front gates about the size of the garden gate) gone, & upon search being made discovered them perched upon the monument in the centre of the <u>campus</u>!! On another occasion they discovered <u>Merchants signs</u> perched up before their houses, as for example Mr. [William J.] Rivers found the sign of a grocer (he lives in the same house as Mr. LaBorde) & it was marked "Rivers & Laborde [sic] Wholesale and Retail Grocers," & Mr. Barnwell got the sign of a shoe and hat store, &c.!! Several persons were fooled, & called on them to buy goods. . . !![10]

Even before Townsend wrote these lines to the folks back home, on October 16, 1870, he was elected to membership in the Euphradian Society, one of two social groups dominating student life, the other being the Clariosophic Society. The societies were essentially debating clubs. Members met each Saturday afternoon at five o'clock to ponder such weighty subjects as dueling, foreign immigration to the South, woman suffrage, Mormons, polygamy in Utah, Indian rights to the soil, and whether the minds of the sexes were equally endowed. Not surprisingly, Euphradians did not believe dueling endangered society, opposed the vote for women, thought Mormons should be expelled and polygamy abolished, were scornful of both Indian rights and the female mind, and, at least in theory, favored foreign immigrants. A question debated in November 1871—"Should seduction be capitally punished?"—apparently was too hot to handle; the minutes indicate no consensus was reached concerning this matter.[11]

Although it is impossible to know just how Belton O'Neall Townsend viewed these topics, Euphradian Society records reveal he quickly became a very active member. Early in 1871 he was named to the finance committee and soon became a monthly orator and then vice president. The Euphradian Society had about twenty members, roughly one-third of the entire student body. During these weeks the group voted to remove the portrait of Professor Barnwell, who was also president of the college, from its hall on the third floor of Harper College. The reason for this action is unclear, but it seems a rather daring move. The members invited Jefferson Davis, who soon would visit Columbia, to attend a meeting.[12]

By November 1871 Townsend, not quite seventeen, was president pro tem and head of a committee conferring with rival Clariosophics concerning occasional joint meetings. On February 29, 1872, following his installation as president, he delivered an inaugural address entitled "The Decadence & Corruption of English Poetical Literature." Whether he or the secretary was responsible, minutes became much fuller at this point, amid demands that, before each meeting, the hall be swept, glass shades washed, and spittoons cleaned. During the remainder of the spring term, Townsend also served as "first critic" and monthly orator, entertaining the society with "an eloquent and edifying address" on May 18.[13]

On the debit side, it should be noted that during his freshman year this young man was fined ten cents on three occasions for "impropriety" and once had to pay $1.50 for failure to perform as monthly orator. However, these juvenile indiscretions are over-shadowed by this entry in the minutes for October 30, 1872: "It has been universally remarked that our young member Mr. B. O. Townsend has improved both his delivery and fluency very much during the present session. He displays[,] whenever he arises, both a thorough research among the classics and a sound & candid judgment whenever he occupies the societies [sic] time." Basking in this praise, Townsend arose and delivered poetry of his own composition entitled "The Inauguration Day of 1873."[14]

Just a few years later Townsend would criticize such societies for their exclusiveness, suggesting that he had faced great difficulties. In *The Atlantic Monthly* he would claim:

> [T]he secret fraternities fell into the hands of aristocratic students who excluded all others. Their organizations were then used to control elections in the literary and debating societies, to which all the students belonged, and in the classes. The high offices were given to aristocrats, and aristocrats were appointed to deliver the valedictories and salutatories. If a plebeian student of talent made himself prominent, cold water was thrown on all he did, and it was not unlikely, if he gave promise of winning the first honors or other high prizes, that such a cry would be raised against him as to cause his withdrawal from the race, if not from college.[15]

Nonetheless, Townsend continued to hold positions of importance during his senior year (1872-73) and even was chosen president once more, although, because of an internal struggle, he never took office. This fight involved re-instatement of two Republican politicians—U.S. Senator Thomas J. Robertson and Governor Franklin J. Moses Jr.—to honorary membership, both having been expelled in April 1868. This proposal, which Townsend favored, came up again and again during the spring of 1873 but always was tabled or ruled out of order. Angered by such tactics, he resigned from the society on three occasions, only to return twice and be re-admitted. Townsend and his friends stressed that, because of the changing composition of the student body, sentiment regarding Robertson and Moses fluctuated through the years; in addition, the two men had enjoyed only honorary status, and expulsion under such conditions was "utterly unwarranted." Frustrated by repeated parliamentary maneuvers, on May 24, shortly before graduating, Townsend resigned for a third and final time. During these same weeks the Euphradians extended honorary membership to Republican stalwart R. B. Carpenter, who agreed to be the society's annual orator.[16]

Following graduation, Townsend returned home to Society Hill where, for about six months, he worked on an epic poem, which at that time bore the title "Paradise Restored." Over fifty pages of notes assembled for this undertaking overflow with classical allusions and cite the writings of Shakespeare, Byron, Goldsmith, Keats, Milton, Tennyson, Dryden, Dante, Spencer, Burns, and Bryant, as well as those of Christopher Columbus, Thomas Jefferson, Benjamin Franklin, Marshal Ney, and Rufus Choate. In all, some seventy individuals are mentioned, plus the Bible. This prodigious research would produce, a decade later, a rambling account, in verse, of Reconstruction in South Carolina entitled "Wild with All Regret."[17]

In addition to doing battle with rhymed couplets, Townsend also was locked in a father-son struggle with the elder Townsend, scornful of a literary career, nudging the younger toward law books. The major's logic eventually prevailed, although not immediately, for his son obviously continued to polish his poems and compose essays. This breach, according to family tradition, was so intense that, although living in the same house in Society Hill, Major B. D. Townsend and Belton did not speak to each other for nearly a year. Only in January 1877 would Belton be admitted to the bar after studying with his cousin, J. Knox Livingston, a young, Florida-born attorney who had settled in Bennettsville in May 1870. Eventually Townsend would form a partnership, Townsend, Livingston, and Townsend, with Livingston and another cousin, Charles P. Townsend. Livingston would serve two terms in the lower house of the General Assembly in the 1880s and 1890s, represent Marlboro County in the state senate (1899-1902), and make an unsuccessful bid to become lieutenant governor in 1900.[18]

### "A SOUTHERN CAMP"

Sometime late in 1874, Townsend dispatched a manuscript to the offices of the prestigious *Atlantic Monthly* in Boston. The subject of these writings is unclear, but on December 19 editor William Dean Howells returned the material with both regrets and encouragement. He praised the critical thinking, found the topic "well thought out," and said Townsend's work showed "promise of success." Yet the over-all effect was too much an imitation of Thomas Babington Macaulay. Howells advised the young man to "avoid cramming into every point all you know about it, adduce nothing that does not throw the strongest light on it." In short, be more direct and write in simple terms. Howells then added a few phrases that would have unforeseen consequences for both editor and writer: "But you are so far from literary centres, why do you not employ yourself with some other sort of writing? I have asked many Southerners to write something about the present social state of their section—and quite vainly. Can't you do this for at least one neighborhood of your State? Pray think of it."[19]

Inspired by this response, Townsend evidently abandoned the study of law during the ensuing months, for in the spring of 1876 Howells received a book-length analysis of the troubled South Carolina scene. On June 14, 1876, the *Atlantic Monthly* editor informed Townsend that the material was much too voluminous for magazine use. He had considered offering it to a book publisher, but times were "so hard" he thought that useless. Instead, he was about to return the manuscript when he picked it up and perused a few pages. He wrote:

> I read the whole chapter then, because it was so interesting I could not leave it off. It is simply wonderful in its fullness and closeness, and the style is generally very simple and good. I accept that chapter, and I beg you to leave the Ms with me a little longer, for I think I <u>may</u> be able to use it all next year. Shall I publish the matter with your name? I thought it might cause you trouble … and I will keep the authorship secret if you wish.[20]

Actually, as events unfolded, Howells did not publish these precise words, and his correspondence with Townsend took a strange turn. For some reason, a photograph of the aspiring writer, then twenty-one years old, was sent north, and on July 11 the Boston editor wrote to Townsend's mother expressing great surprise:

> His face, like his writing, interests me very much. Isn't he quite young? Or was this picture taken some years ago? There is so much close and careful observation in what he has sent me, and the spirit of his work is so candid and quick that I can hardy believe the photograph is a recent one—that such a boyish figure is that of so sober a worker[.]
>
> I trust that no harm may come to him from the entire freedom with which he has written of the life about him, and I shall be careful to guard his incognito.[21]

Then, a few months later, amid confusion and embarrassment, Howells wrote that some chapters may have been returned to Society Hill by mistake. If this had happened, he suggested Townsend revise them in light of recent events, referring to the hotly contested Rutherford B. Hayes and Samuel J. Tilden campaign for the presidency and the battle being waged for control of South Carolina. He expressed sincere regret for this error, noting Townsend's last letter arrived too late to be used by the *Atlantic Monthly* before the election and he had sent it on to the *New York Tribune*.[22]

Five days later, Howells forwarded copies of two extensive articles published in that influential daily on October 14 and 16, both entitled "A Southern Camp." The first, nearly four columns long and complemented by a scathing editorial, carried a subhead stressing intimidation. The second, a bit shorter, talked openly of anarchy and disorder. Howells emphasized that he supplied editor Whitelaw Reid with Townsend's name and address, "about which I charged him to be very careful." And Reid kept the secret well, crediting authorship to "a white native of the State who is not a Republican."[23]

In the *Tribune*, Townsend wrote that South Carolina was then an "armed camp," and anarchy reigned throughout the land. Townsend's analysis of the situation went something like this: Those who led the secession movement were thoroughly discredited by defeat and, as a rule, played little or no political role for nearly a decade. With the demise of the corrupt carpetbag government and election in 1874 of Governor Daniel H. Chamberlain—a northern Republican who had lived in the state since 1866, served as attorney general (1868-70), and was a true reformer—a golden age seemed at hand: "The negroes were free, enfranchised, and undisturbed in their rights, and yet the whites were conscientiously protected from plunder and high taxes."[24] (The South Carolina Republican Party was the party of Lincoln, supported by most African Americans, but by few native whites, who stood by the Democratic Party.)

But the emergence during that same year of a large Democratic majority in the U.S. House of Representatives (which included in its ranks very vocal ex-Confederates) stirred the latent fire-eater spirit, as did the Democratic take-over of Mississippi by shotgun and revolver. Soon intemperate Democratic organs appeared in Greenville and Charleston attacking any form of cooperation with Republicans. And, when the Democrats held their state convention in August 1876, the "straight-outs" (those who opposed any compromise with the Republicans) prevailed by a narrow margin, even though many in the party continued to express faith in Chamberlain. In fact, until the day Wade Hampton III was nominated by the Democrats, the powerful Charleston *News and Courier* actively backed the Republican governor's bid for re-election. In the opinion of Townsend, wherever blacks were in the majority, whites seemed content with the Chamberlain administration.

To counter what straight-outs viewed as treason, their leaders—notably Matthew Calbraith Butler and Martin W. Gary, both of Edgefield County—began to stir the racial cauldron. In their determination to sow discord, they often were aided by discredited Democrats, men tainted by personal involvement with carpetbag corruption who sensed an opportunity to regain status and power. The result was a series of tragic incidents, outrages, and murders—in fact, all-out race war in some communities.

It was reminiscent, wrote Townsend, of 1860 when no Southerner dared give voice to Union sentiment. Each individual must conform or face the consequences, and some endeavored to demonstrate personal sincerity by outdoing their comrades in violence. One hears much of the intimidation of blacks, he conceded, but in his view it was intimidation of whites that rendered the former possible. And, in contrast to what many historians have written in the past century, Townsend placed much of the blame for what was transpiring squarely on the shoulders of Wade Hampton, the man heading up the straight-out ticket—"the aristocrat of the aristocrats, the fire-eater of the fire-eaters, a famous general in the Confederate army, the reincarnation of Calhounism, Jeff. Davisism, anti-Northism, and Southern intolerance."

Townsend stressed that Hampton was as much a Mississippian as a South Carolinian and he closed his first article on this note: "Hampton was in Mississippi prior to the last election there, which the Democrats carried by the shot-gun policy. The similarities of the methods employed by the Democrats in the canvass going on here now, with Hampton as their leader, forces me to the conclusion that the experiment is to be repeated here."

The second *Tribune* article was largely an expansion of themes found in the first, plus tales of a few blacks paraded about as Democratic converts and the story of a Charleston riot in which blacks more than held their own. After all, Townsend observed, this is "a game two can play at." But his opening thoughts about fire-eaters formed perhaps the most intriguing sequence. The dream of Democratic resurgence had, in his words, "driven the old Bourbon element at the South into a species of insanity." They talked of electing the Democrat Tilden, carrying Congress, and running the nation as in the days of old. And by this South Carolinians meant with their leaders, men with the stature of John C. Calhoun, William Campbell Preston, William Lowndes, George McDuffie, and Robert Y. Hayne. According to Townsend, the fire-eaters believed "The Confederacy failed . . . because South Carolina was not allowed to direct its councils—because [Jefferson] Davis and not [Robert Barnwell] Rhett was made President." They are "crazed," he added, by their desire to go to Washington and turn things, politically and socially, upside down, this being, next to putting down the Negro, their primary goal.[25]

Local reaction to these articles was surprisingly mild, possibly because few South Carolinians read New York papers or perhaps they were much too engrossed in events swirling about them. In a lengthy editorial, the *News and Courier* denied much of what appeared in the first article, stating that the writer, whoever he was, "grossly represents the facts." Contradicting Townsend, editor Francis W. Dawson claimed there were no artillery parades in the state, Hampton was not wealthy (in fact, he owned no property, "none whatsoever"), and there was no evidence of widespread intimidation, at least not of the sort alleged by the *Tribune*.[26]

This journal vowed once more that Hampton, its new-found friend, would be elected, and under his administration South Carolina would enjoy true democracy, white and black living "contentedly" together:

> There will be no violence or lawlessness, and no proscription. School-houses will spring up all over the State. The wheels of trade will move with ever-increasing rapidity. And in a few years the horror and shame of the days of Scott, and Moses, and Chamberlain, will be as a fading dream. The result—Peace, Justice, Honor—is all the people crave. For that alone do the "fire-eaters" of South Carolina give brain and sinew, without stint, to the Democratic cause.[27]

Much more important than this blather and bluster is what happened the same day these words appeared in print—President Ulysses S. Grant's decision to dispatch federal troops to South Carolina to restore order. What role Townsend's "Southern Camp" articles played in this drama is not known, but it is quite possible they achieved some effect in Washington. Within a few weeks, elections were held amid fraud and deceit on both sides, followed by harsh words, and—for several months—dual government in South Carolina, Chamberlain and Hampton each claiming he was governor. The *New York Times* reported that, while addressing a crowd in Columbia on December 14, Matthew Gary vowed there would be no violence until Hampton ordered Democrats to act. But, when it started, he said the faithful should "commence with Chamberlain and shoot down."[28]

## ESSAYS OF "A SOUTH CAROLINIAN"

Details such as these and much more also can be found in four essays Townsend published in the *Atlantic Monthly* during the next year or so. Although basically political in nature, they also delve into South Carolina history, morals, culture, economics, social life, and race relations—virtually every aspect of the contemporary scene. The first and longest, "The Political Condition of South Carolina," appeared in February 1877, followed by "South Carolina Morals" in April, "South Carolina Society" in June, and "The Result in South Carolina," the lead article in the issue for January 1878. Each was signed simply "A South Carolinian."

In "The Political Condition," Townsend begins by blasting the corruption within the Republican Party. "From 1868 to 1874 inclusive," he concludes, "the government of South Carolina was a grand carnival of crime and debauchery." But then, he explains, the Klan arose, and "their excesses soon carried the score over on the other side." The bulk of the article itemizes offenses, often brutal, caused by whites against blacks: lynchings, beatings, threats, intimidation, and economic reprisals. He describes confrontations and riots throughout the state: in Hamburg, Cainhoy, Charleston, and Ellenton. Remarkably, at a time when South Carolina was so dramatically split, Townsend criticizes all: Democrat and Republican, white and black, wealthy and poor.[29]

In his second essay he attempts to understand the morals that allowed such depredations to occur, writing in a more philosophical than reportorial manner, and again he is lavish with his critique. In his analysis he anticipates W. J. Cash's *The Mind of the South* (1941). Neither white nor black, he writes, has much respect for the law, but whites especially disregard it in any issue concerning blacks. "To swallow an insult from a negro would be perpetual infamy" to a white man, he claims. "Accordingly, the whites do not think it wrong to shoot, stab, or knock down negroes on slight provocation. It is actually thought a great point, among certain classes, to be able to boast that one has killed or beaten a negro." Ironically, one of the qualities of Southerners that he condemns is their drunkenness, which "is deplorably prevalent to this day."[30]

In his third essay, "South Carolina Society," Townsend again waxes philosophical, discussing the different elements of the social structure. He distinguishes between the majority of African Americans and those who have accumulated some wealth and have been elected to office. Among whites he names "the aristocracy, the respectable people, the working people, and the poor whites or sand-hillers." He provides fascinating details about daily life—clothing, housing, food, entertainment, and, especially, black-white relations. He is particularly critical of low-income blacks (their food "is coarse and barbarously prepared," their homes "are dens of filth, giving off an intolerable stench," their clothing "is simply disgusting") and whites ("squalid, lazy, and extremely ignorant"). Townsend was certainly as bigoted as most other whites of his generation. In fact, in his second essay, he writes, "The negro (not standing very high anyhow biologically) is, when aroused, a wild beast. There is not the slightest doubt that in the use of the handy billy and the torch he is an expert of the first order; and it is probable that in the murder of women and children he can equal the Indian." He was hardly an apologist for the Republican Party or African Americans in general. And yet he was so repulsed by the political violence against blacks as to call attention to it.[31]

The initial onslaught in the *Atlantic,* not surprisingly, stirred the greatest reaction. On February 7, the *News and Courier* termed it "a sketch remarkable for its skilful [sic] duplicity and malignant cunning." "So interwoven in this article is fact and fiction, truth and falsehood, and so malevolent its tone, under the guise of insinuating candor . . . ," fumed Dawson, "we think it the most slanderous and most pernicious of all the recent publications directed against the South." This editor seemed especially distressed by the portrayal of Chamberlain as a reformer, "and we are informed, for the first time," he wrote, "that he was admitted into the most aristocratic society and lionized everywhere!"[32]

Soon after that, Howells had other concerns. To begin with, Chamberlain—forced out of office by the Compromise of 1877 that gave Republican Hayes the White House and withdrew federal troops from the South, thus paving the way for a resurgence of Democratic power—had figured out that Townsend was the author of the *Atlantic* articles. The first hint came in a memorandum from Frederick Jackson Garrison to Howells on March 22, 1877. Garrison, son of abolitionist William Lloyd Garrison, worked at the offices of H. O. Houghton & Company, which produced the *Atlantic Monthly*. Unaware that Chamberlain and Townsend had met when the latter graduated from college in 1873, Garrison was puzzled: "I can't imagine how he has got at it, or what clue he had to work on." A month later, on April 25, while praising Townsend's third essay, Howells added this note to Garrison, "The Governor sh'd be put off the scent if possible, and in any case begged not to make his guess public. He can understand why."[33]

### "THEY ARE NOT POETRY"

Three days later, Howells turned his attention to yet another matter involving Townsend. Sometime during these weeks, the young South Carolinian dispatched several of his poems to Boston. As diplomatically as possible—opening with the words "My dear friend," instead of the customary "Dear Sir" or "My dear Mr. Townsend"—Howells returned them. "They express," he wrote, "or rather intimate a deep and true feeling, but they are not poetry." Howells was certain that Townsend's future lay in literature, but he doubted that it included poetry. "You have already made an impression in the magazine which few men of your age have done," he continued, "and you have but to go on the course you have taken. I hope to use [one] or two more of your papers. Do you know they have been the subject of wide comment in the North?"[34]

Struggling to strike a positive note, Howells suggested Townsend try his hand at a "very realistic short story of South Carolina life. I am sure you have the material for it." Again he stressed "the simplest work is the best" and added these words of concern: "I earnestly hope that no harm may come to you from your Atlantic papers, which several Southerners have praised to me for their truth."[35]

Five months later, on September 26, Howells requested brief comment on the results of the 1876 election in South Carolina, something comprehensive but "despassionately [sic] stated." Townsend's fourth and final essay of January 1878 closed on a troubling, uncertain note. He said he rejoiced in the end of blatant corruption and the decline of violence; however, the revival of intolerance and strained race relations created widespread unease. Such developments were perplexing, even frightening at times. He did not know how to evaluate the full gamut of change. His mind, he conceded, was "not made up."[36]

If Belton O'Neall Townsend found the world about him confusing, his determination to become a poet was as strong as ever, despite the criticism of his mentor. On June 3, 1878, he dispatched a sample of his work to the dean of American poets, Henry Wadsworth Longfellow, along with a fawning letter apologizing for this intrusion upon his time and seeking help toward publication.

> There are some who believe that a poet's work is not an index of his character. I am not of that opinion: I most sincerely believe, or hope so strongly at least that hope & belief have become confounded, that he who wrote the Arsenal at Springfield, although of the Boston School[,] can see merit in poets outside of the Hub; & although a Northerner can overlook the hard fate which assigned a young author's birth-place to the despised South. And when a half hour's attention from you might save me who has aspired not wisely, but too well, from what promises to be a life-time of lingering torture, it were mockery to make any reference to gratitude.[37]

Within four days a reply was on its way to Townsend, written by Samuel Longfellow, the aging poet's brother and official biographer. The letter, dated June 7, can only be interpreted as a "brush-off." Longfellow said so many manuscripts were sent to him that he could not review all of them. He advised Townsend to publish in regional papers, deal with subjects of local interest ("we write best of things into which we can put our hearts"), and speak not of the "despised South." Although part of the original letter, now in Harvard's Houghton Library, is missing, and the signature has been cut out by an autograph collector, it contains this brief addendum: "P.S. I return your manuscript by today's post, and trust you will not feel hurt that for the reasons given I cannot return it with any opinion of its merits."[38]

## TWENTY-THREE YEAR-OLD ATTORNEY

This rebuff, the second in as many years, may have sobered Townsend somewhat—at least he seems to have turned to law books and community affairs with new vigor. Eight weeks earlier, in March 1878, at age twenty-three, he opened an office in Florence and quickly became a prominent fixture in the everyday life of that community (population then about two thousand). In addition to the normal flow of briefs, deeds, wills, and court appearances, he soon headed up two building-and-loan associations, a Masonic lodge, and a fire company. He worshipped frequently at St. John's Episcopal Church. His principal social interest was, however, a public library and reading room that grew rapidly under his leadership. With the help of benefits such as railway excursions to Lake Waccamaw and performances of *East Lynne* and Gilbert and Sullivan's *H.M.S. Pinafore* (with Townsend playing leading roles), the collection grew to some four thousand volumes by 1884. On August 1, 1882, in an article entitled "Flourishing Florence," the *News and Courier* said, for the success of this undertaking, "all honor is due to Belton O. Townsend, Esq., the little Hercules when anything like work is to be done."[39]

During the first year or so of active practice, Townsend served as counsel for two railroads, then, distressed by corporate insensitivity, reversed field and represented those injured by his former clients. This stance, coupled with eloquence and wit, made this young attorney an obvious nominee for public office. Although reluctant at first, in 1883 he agreed to seek the post of intendant (mayor) of Florence. The result was a showdown between railroad muscle and those who feared such power, his opponent being Captain W. H. Day, master railroad car builder, Confederate veteran, and the highest-ranking official of the Wilmington, Columbia & Augusta Railroad living in Florence. In a lengthy letter to voters, published in a supplement to the *Florence Times*, Townsend outlined his position on several key issues. If elected, his first goal would be to form a new county with Florence as its seat of government; his second, "to start, encourage, and promote a spirit of general public enterprise and improvements in Florence beneficial to its growth and prosperity...."[40]

This all sounds reasonable enough, but the true battle in a community where half the voters were railroad workers centered on the interests of their employers. Much of the railroad property in the Florence area was exempt from local taxation, and many expected the railroads soon would ask the town to go into debt to build a new line to Wilson, North Carolina. Unfortunately for Townsend, his statement of goals included less-than-complimentary allusions to nearby county seats such as Marion, Darlington, and Kingstree, "obscure villages at a distance (which have missed their legitimate province as good cotton fields)." There residents of his proposed county had to record deeds and transact business "at vast inconvenience and expense."[41]

These words, interpreted as an affront by some, plus railroad money and coercion, led to Townsend's defeat, 265-215. Perhaps it was unwise to transform a local race into a referendum on a new county. In any case, the railroads made certain their man would prevail and the result was a lively affair indeed. The *Pee Dee Index* said the *Florence Times* described the balloting in this fashion: "It is with regret that we are unable to report a quiet and peaceable election, and on the contrary, there were fights, rioting, and disorder, in which clubs, bricks, and knives were freely used, and to which the bandaged heads of a dozen individuals will attest. That this should exist when no politics are in the question, is unfortunate, and speaks little to the credit of the town."[42] Just where Townsend—5 feet, 5 inches, 120 pounds—was in the midst of this mayhem is not known. This would be his only political venture. However, in the process, he raised an issue that refused to fade away: the creation of a new county.

## "IT CAN ONLY DO YOU HARM"

But soon the ex-politician was again a poet. On February 22, 1884, Belton O'Neall Townsend completed work on a lengthy manuscript and shipped it off to a Columbia printer, Charles S. Calvo Jr. Unfortunately, much like the injudicious references to neighboring towns, it quickly got him into hot water. The poems, assembled over many years and produced at the author's expense, were dedicated and addressed to William Dean Howells, clearly without permission: "Not only am I indebted to you more than to any other literary friend for assistance, kindness and attention, but also for frequent encouraging and flattering expressions. . . ." The opening lines—by careful selection of phrases—created the impression that he wrote with the encouragement of both Howells and Longfellow, which was patently untrue.

*Plantation Lays and Other Poems* appeared about ten weeks later, early in May 1884. Townsend, bursting with pride, quickly dispatched copies in all directions—to Howells, the Euphradian Society ("from one of its old members, and ex-President"), President Chester A. Arthur, Jefferson Davis, local politicians such as U.S. Senator Matthew C. Butler, and various newspapers and magazines throughout the nation. He even sent copies overseas to British Prime Minister William Gladstone and poet Algernon Charles Swinburne.[43] Today one can find copies in the collections of many institutions, including the Library of Congress and Oxford University's Bodleian Library.

Of the 108 pages in this slim volume, almost half are made up of the epic "Wild with All Regret: A Tale of Reconstruction," on which Townsend had been working for so many years. A sense of the poem's rhythm can be gained from the opening lines: "I'll not invoke the Muses, / But with a sheriff's sale, / A very homely matter, / You may think, will start my tale." The sheriff's sale concerns a fictional plantation called "The Oaks" (not the actual Middleton family plantation of the same name) and a "set of sharks who waited, / On every day of sale, / During all of Reconstruction, / Round the court house steps and jail, / In hopes to catch a bargain, / And for a farthing buy / The home of widows, orphans, / And turn them 'neath the sky." Characters include the beautiful and pure Allie, her aged and loyal nurse Chloe, her beloved and courageous Willie (who eventually joins with other "red-clad horsemen," clearly Wade Hampton's Redshirts, to avenge her), and the scoundrel Republican, Whitmire. Unlike his prose, there is no condemnation of the anti-black violence in the state, only of the misdeeds of the cruel Republicans. And unlike the *Atlantic* and the *New York Tribune* articles, which had described him as "not a Republican," now his "Biographical Introduction," distributed with copies of the book, said he always voted with the Democratic Party, "though he is not a partisan, but independent and has declined with aversion any association with the corrupt Independent and Republican parties in this State."[44]

For the most part, *Plantation Lays* elicited mild local comment, most of it laudatory. The *News and Courier* said the president of the Darlington Reading Club praised Townsend as one who possessed "a rare power of word painting and gave promise of future progress in the art of writing." Five days later, the Charleston daily conceded, "there will probably be some difference of opinion as to the merit of the poems," while pointing with pride to one of special interest, "The Charleston Fairy."[45]

The *Columbia Register* noted the book, "produced in handsome form" by Calvo (who also published the *Register*), was on sale at Bryan's bookstore. However, this daily added that the *Washington Post*, although it found "merits of versification and sentiment" in Townsend's lines, said the work would scarcely entitle the author to high marks as a poet. A rather lengthy review in the *Carolina Spartan* concluded with the observation that "those who wish a book Southern all over and all through should secure a copy of these poems." And *The Nation* struck a similar chord, noting such themes were much in vogue:

> … it is a curious fact that, while the social prejudice against the negro is greater than against the Indian, the literary interest is in inverse ratio, so that "Uncle Remus" is popular while the aboriginal legends fall dead. The circular accompanying the book gives an ample biography of the author, perhaps a little anticipating the march of fame. Mr. Townsend has, we believe, done some good work in prose,

but we cannot find his verse to be far above mediocrity, though his themes are sometimes fresh and his moral often good....[46]

The reaction in far-off New England was more immediate, clearly defined, and much stronger in tone. On May 14 Howells wrote Townsend and administered what can only be interpreted as a verbal spanking:

> My dear friend,
>
> It was extremely pleasant to see your handwriting again, and to know that you still valued our old relation. But I cannot mar the recollection of that by praising your volume of verse, which is as wholly bad as a thing of this kind can be. I regret that you have printed it, and it can only do you harm with those who do not know the good work you have done in other directions. I desire the smallest currency for it. You must forgive my frankness: I should have been less your friend if I had forborne.[47]

Ten days later, Howells received this jocular note from his friend Samuel Clemens (Mark Twain):

> Good land, have you seen the "poems" of that South Carolinian idiot, "Belton O'Neall Townsend, A. B. & Attorney at Law"?—& above all, the dedication of them to you?
> If you _did_ write him what he says you did, you richly deserve hanging; & if you didn't, _he_ deserves hanging,—But he deserves hanging any-way & in any & all cases—no, boiling, gutting, brazing in a mortar—no, no, there _is_ no death that can meet his case. Now think of this literary louse dedicating his garbage to you, & quoting encouraging compliments from you & poor dead Longfellow. Let us hope there is a hell, for this poets [sic] sake, who carries his bowels in his skull, & when they operate works the discharge into rhyme & prints it.
> Ah, if he had only dedicated this diarrhea to [Thomas Bailey] Aldrich, I could just howl with delight; but the joke is lost on you—just about wasted.[48]

Responding to Clemens immediately, on May 26, Howells tried to explain what had happened:

> That incredible wretch wrote some of the most striking papers I

ever printed in the Atlantic—full of careful, sound observation, and simply and well written. They were prose. He sent me 'poetry,' and I sent it back, warning him against it in plain language as trash. I have written him to the same effect since his book came out, but the public can never understand that I did not endorse his poetry....

I could not explain how I came to praise Townsend's prose without ruining him in the community where he lives. So, you see, he <u>had</u> me.[49]

Sometime during the summer months, Townsend replied to the stern rebuke handed him by Howells, apparently expressing keen disappointment and complaining of ill health. On August 30 Howells tried to close the breach created by *Plantation Lays*. Grieved to hear of Townsend's "sufferings," he said he hoped his young friend was well again and perhaps could see the May letter in a different light. "If I wounded you, you must forgive me; the thought of giving pain to any one is intolerable to me; and I have truly liked and respected you in spite of what I consider still the error of publishing your poems. I should be wronging you very cruelly to praise them; but—I like you so much—you seem to me so true and good and grave in spirit—that I wish with all my heart I could praise them."[50]

During these same weeks, publisher Calvo produced a little brochure designed to boost sales of *Plantation Lays*. Of about a hundred reviews and comments received, many of them "flattering beyond all expectation," only three, he said, were unfavorable. Calvo promised a second edition in the near future; meanwhile, copies would be "sent by mail, postpaid, on receipt of $1.25 each; usual discount to Booksellers."[51]

This promotional piece contains quotations from daily papers in Chicago, New York, St. Louis, Charleston, etc., as well as yet another patchwork quote by Howells—lines lifted from his letters of July 11, 1876, and April 28, 1877, the first written to Townsend's mother, the second to Townsend rejecting his poems. There is a brief quotation from Longfellow concerning the merits of Townsend's work, and positive comments from Jefferson Davis and South Carolinians George Walton Williams, Edward McCrady Jr., B. H. Rutledge, Col. W. L. Trenholm, and J. H. Carlisle, president of Wofford College. One of the longest blurbs presents anonymous praise by "an Eminent (Living) American Author and Public Man," who urged Townsend to shake the dust of South Carolina from his shoes. "Come, and dwell North; your native section is not the home of letters. Let your future editions of Plantation Lays issue from some of our mammoth Northern houses, who will send them forth in a halo of light and publicity, and whose very name imprinted on your title page will secure you at once the reading and attention your merits will afterwards commands [sic]...." Such talent, this unnamed admirer continued, would be buried in the South and soon forgotten. Look at what happened to Edgar Allan Poe and Henry Timrod. Profit by their example and do not become "a mute inglorious Milton."[52]

Clearly the admonishment administered in mid-May by Howells had little effect. Belton O'Neall Townsend continued to misquote both Howells and Longfellow and perhaps composed the lines attributed to "an eminent (living) American author and public man." No second edition of *Plantation Lays* ever appeared. This apparently was the end of the young attorney's literary career, although he contributed bits and pieces to the *News and Courier* from time to time.[53]

However, Townsend's life may have inspired another writer—his old friend William Dean Howells. In February 1886 *Century Magazine* began publication in serial form of Howell's "The Minister's Charge; or, the Apprenticeship of Lemuel Barker." In eleven installments, the story recounts the life of a country boy, determined to become a poet, who shows some of his verses to a vacationing Boston clergyman. The minister, to the distress of his wife and despite his own better judgment, half-heartedly praises the young man's work. Encouraged, the youth sends several verses of a long poem to him and requests help finding a publisher. When there is no reply, Lemuel Barker appears in Boston and the minister is forced to speak his mind. Too embarrassed to return home, Barker is plunged into a series of metropolitan adventures, during which he commits the same sin as the minister, not speaking the truth about a dishonest associate, an oversight that causes him much grief.

Biographers of Howells indicate he began this tale as a series of short stories in 1883, let it languish when he turned to other matters (including reading proofs of *The Rise of Silas Lapham*), and then took it up once more following the exchange of letters with Townsend. Interestingly, Lem Barker (5 feet, 6 inches, 130 pounds) resembles Townsend, and one of Lem's employers bears the name of Corey, strikingly similar to that of Townsend's brother, Cary.[54] Thus it would appear that only two people benefited from the publication of *Plantation Lays*—the man to whom the work was dedicated (much to his distress) and perhaps publisher Calvo—but not the poet himself.

Townsend's final communication with northern publishers occurred in December 1888 as Houghton Mifflin was preparing an index to the *Atlantic Monthly.* Would he object, the publisher asked, if authorship of his "valuable papers" in volume thirty-nine were revealed? If not, then please explain what the initial "O" stands for. Townsend subsequently supplied his full name.[55]

## MARRIAGE, CHILDREN, AND DEATH

Although poetry and publicity may have dominated this young man's thoughts throughout much of 1884, he also found time to contemplate matrimony. The prospective bride was nineteen-year-old Leah McClenaghan (May 25, 1865-December 29, 1945), granddaughter of a Scots-Irish planter who had resided in the village of Marion on the eve of the Civil War. Her father, Horatio McClenaghan, a farmer, was living in Mars Bluff in 1880 with his wife Amelia, seven children, and an eighty-year-old black servant named Dinah. McClenaghan had served as an officer in Hampton's Legion during the Civil War and was a leader of the Red Shirts in his area in 1876. Leah's grandfather (born in Belfast) and her father both married well, brides whose families owned extensive property; however, after the war they were land poor—in the words of descendant Nick Zeigler, "impoverished gentry."

*Leah McClenaghan Townsend, wife of Belton O'Neall Townsend. Photo courtesy of Benjamin T. Zeigler.*

"Leah," he adds, "got a scholarship to St. Mary's School in Raleigh and was generally reckoned to be exceptionally bright."[56]

Belton and Leah's wedding took place on October 19, 1885, at the Darlington-area home of W. J. Maxwell, husband of one of Leah's relatives. The officiating clergyman was Reverend J. W. Humbert, a local Methodist minister. The young couple immediately departed for Charleston on what was supposed to be a brief "wedding tour." The groom was scheduled to appear in court on October 26, not as an attorney, but as defendant in a criminal suit. A few weeks earlier, on September 30, Townsend shot at (but failed to hit) Thomas W. Norment. This fracas occurred at a dance in Darlington, instigated by Leah's association (flirtation?) with Norment. Words followed and then gunfire. Leah was the only witness. According to family lore, Belton may have persuaded her to marry him so she could not be forced to testify against him in criminal proceedings.[57]

On October 20, while staying at the Charleston Hotel, Townsend received the following telegram from Norment—"Hurrah, accept my congratulations." After discussing the message with friends, he concluded this meant all charges were dropped. Much relieved, Townsend dispatched a wire to Norment, thanking him for his courteous greeting. Under these circumstances, the newlyweds decided to take a month's vacation, instead of a week, and set out for Florida. However, en route, Townsend had second thoughts. What if he had misinterpreted Norment's telegram? Just to be sure, he stopped in Savannah on October 25 and filed an affidavit with a justice of the peace outlining his version of the matter. Whatever Norment's intent, the charges were dropped, although Townsend eventually paid a $200 fine for carrying a concealed weapon.[58]

Upon their return from Florida, the Townsends set up housekeeping about a mile from the center of Florence in a dwelling owned by William Quirk, businessman, saw-mill operator, and in the 1890s railroad station master. A few months later, on the night of June 5-6, 1886, the structure was completely destroyed by fire under bizarre circumstances. At about two in the morning, Leah Townsend thought she heard a cat prowling about the second floor. Taking a kerosene lamp in hand, she went to investigate, whereupon the cat jumped out an open window. Still in pursuit, Leah, who was then pregnant, leaned out the window, only to have the sash suddenly come down, smashing the lamp and scattering kerosene. Flames spread so rapidly that nothing was saved. She and two guests—Jennie and Sandy Evans—fled to nearby woods and watched the blaze from a safe distance. No one came to the scene. Her husband, according to the *Pee Dee Index*, was not at home.[59]

During the next three years, the Townsends would become the parents of three daughters—Mary, Helen, and Leah. Mary (1886-89), born shortly after the fire, died three years later. Helen (1887-1976), schoolteacher and mother of Nick Zeigler, married Eugene Noel Zeigler Sr., an Orangeburg native, who for many years was a railroad conductor. Leah (1889-1981), who never married, became a well-known historian and lawyer. In 1926 she received a master's degree in history from the University of South Carolina, followed three years later by a doctorate, only the second such degree awarded by that institution to a woman. On both occasions, she explored the story of South Carolina Baptists, research published in 1935 and still consulted by scholars. While ill in the mid-1920s, Leah Townsend studied law with her half-brother Peter McEachin, passed the bar exams, and eventually joined him to form the firm of McEachin & Townsend.[60]

In addition to fatherhood and the practice of law, in the late 1880s Belton O'Neall Townsend was much involved in the creation of the new county of Florence, which became a reality on December 22, 1888. He served as secretary of a forty-six-man executive committee formed to accomplish this task and offered a toast to "the judiciary and the bar," one of eleven tendered at a lavish banquet given in Florence on May 1, 1889, to mark the birth of this new entity. The address of welcome on that occasion was delivered by Captain W. H. Day, the man who had rebuffed Townsend at the polls in 1883.[61]

Although Belton O'Neall Townsend was prospering professionally, his home life was less serene, perhaps because of a fondness for liquor. Sometime in February 1891 his wife took their two little girls and, according to the local press, went for a visit "in the country." Later, the *News and Courier* stated more bluntly the obvious truth that the Townsends were living apart, at least temporarily. During these weeks, distraught and unhappy, he talked of suicide and bought a gun, a purchase he subsequently denied and asked the dealer to keep secret.[62]

About sundown on the evening of February 27, neighbors saw him walking about the piazza of his two-story home "in an intoxicated condition." A short time later, a black youth who waited upon Townsend left his employer stretched out in bed reading. Under Townsend's pillow, the youngster later recalled, was the new pistol. At about ten o'clock, again according to neighbors, the light in the bedroom was extinguished, followed by an explosion (or perhaps a pistol shot) and a burst of flames that quickly engulfed the entire structure.[63]

A fire company soon arrived at the scene but could do little to stem the holocaust that ensued. All of the doors in the house were unlocked, except the one leading to Townsend's bedroom, where his badly charred remains were found the next day. There were, of course, rumors of foul play and murder, fueled, it appears, by his

*Leah McClenaghan Townsend, widow of Belton O'Neall Townsend, with their children Helen and Leah. Photo courtesy of Benjamin T. Zeigler.*

brother Cary. However, following an inquest, the *News and Courier* summed up the tragedy in this fashion: "The conclusion of the community is that he set fire to the room, probably having saturated everything with oil, because of the rapid spread of the fire, particularly in his room, and then shot himself." Irony of ironies, this was the same man who, as a fifteen-year-old college student, told his mother he was getting "wonderfully reconciled to kerosene oil" and used it with great care.[64]

It is difficult to know what to make of such a life and death. His widowed mother tended to blame Leah—who subsequently became the wife of Daniel Malloy McEachin (1869-1937)—for not trying harder to save their marriage.[65] Yet his parents were not entirely without fault. They clearly forced their son into the practice of law against his wishes. More than a century later, it is impossible to determine how much of a battle he waged in response to demands that he abandon pen, paper, and the world of literature for the courtroom. But of course Townsend himself bears most of the responsibility for his erratic, and sometimes bizarre, behavior.

What we do know is that Belton O'Neall Townsend wrote superb, incisive prose, perhaps the most revealing passages ever composed in an attempt to shed light upon a controversial period in the history of his native state. And he also produced sincere, meticulously researched if not superior verse, some of it calculated to serve the same purpose.

# A Southern Camp.
# Intimidation in South Carolina.

*New York Tribune,* October 14, 1876

The Whites under Arms—The Democrats Determined To Carry the State Peacably if They Can, but Forcibly if They Must—Wade Hampton's Apprenticeship in Mississippi
*(From a white native of the state who is not a Republican.)*

CHARLESTON, OCT. 6—One passing through South Carolina would imagine that it was in a state of war. It resembles a vast armed camp. On every green and public square the clang of muskets can be heard, as parading infantry ground their arms. From every old field rings out threateningly the note of the bugle or the booming of the field-piece, as cavalry and artillery perform their evaluations. The depots are crowded with cases of firearms, ordered from the North. The stores cannot supply the demand for arms and ammunition, and every gunsmith in the city and blacksmith in the country is repairing dilapidated weapons. No one is seen on the streets without a repeater or rifle; and not a day passes in town or city but that the quick and scattering reports of guns and pistols, used on targets in the vicinity, would lead a stranger to suppose that a skirmish, if not a battle, was in progress around him. Nor is this all. In every part of the State there are monster open-air political mass meetings. These meetings are followed by torchlight parades, or preceded by processions of rifle clubs cavalry, artillery companies, and civilians, marching to the sound of martial music. The speakers, invariably master-spirits of the Lost Cause, arise and deliver the most vehement addresses, denouncing the Republican Administration and the Republican party, State and National, and calling on their hearers to rise. The wildest cheering rings out in response, mixed with the notes of the bands and the crashing of cannon; and the people disperse to their homes with war, war, for their cry—war even to the knife.

What has caused this? If the Democrats are to be trusted, it is a grand uprising of intelligence against ignorance, of wealth against non-taxpaying aggression, of civilization and refinement against barbarism and degradation. Their banners bear the inscriptions of "The Prostrate State Aroused," "Forbearance has Ceased to be a Virtue," "Down with the Thieves," "Home with the Carpet-Bagger," "Honest Government or Death." It is, they say, a repetition of the stirring scenes of 1776; an irrepressible uprising of the people against grinding tyranny and intolerable oppression; against outrageous encroachment on their rights and privileges; a strike for liberty or for death; in short, a second revolution as momentous as that of a century ago. But, they say, it is a revolution this time not against foreign domination and rapacity, but against an intestine foe; against the subjection of class to class, of enlightened property-holding Anglo-Saxons to a horde of African barbarians under the guidance of unprincipled scoundrels from the North.

## REACTION AGAINST CHAMBERLAIN.

Four months ago the quiet of the grave-yard reigned in South Carolina. For the first time since the war the people were contented. The rotten government of the carpet-baggers had passed away. The robber Governor was no longer in power. An honest ruler had been found at last. From the very moment of the installation of Gov. Chamberlain in December, 1874, reform had been the order of the day. He presided over the people with the cold neutrality of an impartial judge. The depredations of the Legislature were forcibly stopped by the veto. The ignorant or corrupt officers of the former administration were relentlessly removed; new and competent men, in half the instances Democrats, were put in their places. The taxes were reduced. The installation of two unscrupulous judges was arbitrarily, though with good reason, prohibited by the Governor.[1] The prostrate State was prostrate no longer; she had been raised from the ground. Her savior had come. D. H. Chamberlain was the man.[2] The whites were grateful, and were loud in their expressions of commendation. Their popular institutions of learning made him their orator. The fashionable

*Daniel H. Chamberlain, governor of South Carolina 1874-76. Photo courtesy of the South Caroliniana Library, University of South Carolina, Columbia.*

clubs and associations extended cordial invitations for him to attend their celebrations and respond to toasts. The gates of society were flung open to him, and the haughtiest member of the old Southern aristocracy—nay, even the ladies—delighted to honor him and to entertain him at their houses. The Democratic papers loudly and generally advocated his reelection. The Mannings, the Perrys, the Kershaws, and the Simontons—the political leaders of the whites—lent their sanction to the idea.[3] And though the corrupt element of the Republican Party—the element which he had so remorselessly thwarted—was bitterly inimical to the measure, yet every thing pointed to his renomination by the Republicans, indorsement [sic] by the Conservatives, and triumphant reëlection to the executive office.

But, wonderful to relate, this man is to-day denounced from every Democratic stump in South Carolina as an unprincipled adventurer, a malicious liar, a ringleader in rascality, a carpet-bagger of the carpet-baggers. They have let slip the dogs of war against him. Verily, a change has come over the spirit of their dream. What student of political science could, four months ago, have ventured to predict that it would come to this?

## SOUTHERN LEADERS UNPOPULAR AFTER THE WAR.

After the downfall of the Confederacy, there was a perceptible reaction in the South against the fire-eaters and leaders of secession. They had given the counsels which had brought distress and ruin upon the country. Hence they were distrusted. Their influence was still more diminished by another circumstance: they were impoverished by the war. They had possessed counties; this land was now so worthless that no one could be found to purchase it. They had owned regiments of slaves; this wealth had melted away like snow fallen in the river. In consequence nine-tenths of the old aristocrats were compelled to go into bankruptcy. This impoverishment, indeed, was not confined to them—it was widespread. But as their wealth had consisted chiefly of the two articles most depreciated by the war—negroes and real estate—they were more directly affected than the mercantile classes, whose property had been more wisely invested. Then, too, they were "gentlemen;" they had been bred in indolence and dissipation, and knew not how to go to work—how to accommodate themselves to their altered circumstances. Accordingly they remained poor, with few exceptions, while their plebeian neighbors went to work and improved their fortunes. South Carolina has been very quiet ever since the war. The Ku-Klux excitement is the only thing of magnitude which has disturbed the peace, although the State was known as the Prostrate State, ground under foot by carpet-bag rascality and negro domination. The whites, thoroughly disgusted with politics, remained at home and attended to their business. Hundreds have not voted since the war, and thousands have not voted more than once or twice. When they voted they compromised with the Republican party instead of running a straight-out Democratic ticket; they would cast their ballots for honest Republicans, who would bolt the corrupt party nominations. They did this not only in town and county elections, but in three successive State elections. The Republicans liked this, and bolting became a frequent thing. Now under the administration of Chamberlain the assent of the whites to this compromise policy had become well-nigh universal. The races were beginning to trust each other. I have been delighted to see how readily they would support each other for office, voting for tickets on which half the candidates were black and half white, or half Republican and half Conservative. They were beginning to sit together on juries as a matter of course; no remark was made when a colored man took a seat in a first-class car, and in all things each race was learning to treat the other with proper consideration.

It is true that the political leaders of the whites—those sent to the party conventions—were still aristocrats, for the aristocracy includes most Southerners capable of leadership. But then they were mainly new men, from the younger branches of the old families, and whether new or old had, perforce, to conform to the powerful public sentiment of their party. Hence the political conventions of the South Carolina Democracy acted sensibly and moderately, so strong since the war has been the desire of the body of the whites to avoid conflict and to accept the situation. If I am not mistaken, the bombardment of Charleston had something to do with this, and the march of Sherman from the seacoast to North Carolina. It broke the faith Carolinians had reposed in themselves—showed them, so long accustomed to plantation despotism, that they themselves had a master who could tread them down with a heel of iron. Hence the terrible display of the Ku-Klux when Merrill and his soldiery were sent among them;[4] hence the efficiency of United States troops to preserve order in localities where they are quartered, and, consequently, the eagerness of the white Republicans and negroes to call on the National Government for protection whenever they are molested by the Democrats.

## EFFECT OF DEMOCRATIC SUCCESS.

Gov. Chamberlain's administration, then, for a year and a half was the golden era of South Carolina politics. The negroes were free, enfranchised and undisturbed in their rights, and yet the whites were conscientiously protected from plunder and high taxes. But Gov. Chamberlain had not been in power a year when the XLIVth Congress assembled at Washington.

The great tidal wave of 1874 had sent a large Democratic majority to the House of Representatives and prominent among that majority were many ex-Confederate generals. From the very moment it met I noticed an unusual, though carefully concealed, agitation among the fire-eating aristocracy of this State. For years their occupation had been gone. Discarded in politics, out of office, they had been compelled to keep the noiseless tenor of their way along the cool, sequestered vale of private life. But their pride, it seems, had not fallen with their fortunes. They had been compelled to keep quiet; they complied against their wills, and held to their old opinions. They bitterly reflected that they had seen better days, and nursed their wrath to keep it warm. But now a ray of hope dawned on them. They heard of Ben Hill defending Andersonville and Jefferson Davis in the Congress of the United States.[5] They saw Southerners once more holding up their heads in the national capital. They could hardly trust their senses. And then they looked around them: all the Southern States were once more Democratic except South Carolina and Louisiana. These States alone had Republican Governors and negro Legislatures. They alone had not their Stephenses, Gordons, Lamars, Hills, and Proctor Knotts in Congress.[6] Then they reflected on Mississippi—how her 30,000 negro majority had been transformed into 30,000 Democratic majority by the use of the shot-gun and revolver.[7] It was true that they had been relieved from oppression; that their confessed debt to their reform Governor was yet unpaid, and that while they supported him, as in the past, there was no danger of misgovernment. But should they rest content with this? Why not get the upper hand at home, and then make a desperate attempt to seize on the reins of power at Washington?

## THE FIRE-EATERS' CHANGE OF BASE.

The fruits of such thoughts soon began to appear. A violent Democratic daily was established in Greenville—a section of the State where the whites outnumber the colored people.[8] It began a series of the most outrageous onslaughts against Gov. Chamberlain, and accompanying these were the most vehement exhortations for the whites to arouse and shake off their lethargy, and follow in the wake of Alabama and Mississippi. Very soon in several of the adjacent counties—the old Ku-Klux counties where the negroes are in the minority—the whites became, during the Spring of this year, estranged from Gov. Chamberlain and opposed to the compromise policy. But despite its efforts the majority of the whites (all those living in counties where the negroes predominated) remained content with things as they were. And this, too, although a Columbia daily joined in the advocacy of the blood-and-thunder policy.[9] The influence of The Charleston News and Courier had much to do with this. It was then the only daily published in Charleston, was by all odds the leading journal of the State, perhaps of the South, and had a circulation ten times as great as that of the straight-out organs combined. It was found necessary to establish a fire-eating daily in Charleston; so The Journal of Commerce appeared in May. It was intemperate past all expression in advocating its views; and, as soon as possible, the duelist, R. Barnwell Rhett, Jr., formerly editor of The Charleston Mercury and New-Orleans Picayune, was installed as editor. He is the son of the famous R. Barnwell Rhett, Sr., lately deceased, ex-Senator of the United States from South Carolina, the most ultra Southerner that ever breathed, the man to whose efforts above all others is to be attributed the passage of the ordinance of secession, the rival of Jefferson Davis for the Presidency of the Confederate States. The son is like the father.[10]

In the mean time came the celebration of the Fort Moultrie Centennial in Charleston.[11] This was to South Carolina what the Bunker Hill Centennial was to Massachusetts. The aristocrats made it a real old-time Southern revival. All the rifle clubs (then only a dozen in number) in the State, together with an equal number from Georgia and elsewhere, were present. Gen. Wade Hampton was put in command. Thousands and tens of thousands of visitors thronged the city from every part of the State. There were two military companies from the North, but the leaders succeeded in exhibiting to the people of South Carolina the spectacle of thousands of Confederate troops once more under arms, with Wade Hampton for their captain. This produced a profound sensation, and touched chords in many a South Carolinian's bosom. Then the speeches were full of the past glories of the State: of her prowess during the war, of her wrongs since the war, and of her future when she should be relieved from thralldom. There were many colored policemen in South Carolina,

*Matthew Calbraith Butler, a major figure in the Hamburg Massacre, later elected to the U.S. Senate. Photo courtesy of the South Caroliniana Library, University of South Carolina, Columbia.*

whom the whites here had learned to treat properly; indeed, they were so common as to attract no notice. But the troops from Democratic Georgia were startled at such a novelty as negroes holding offices, even so humble as positions on the police. So they were loud in their derision, made over them ruthlessly, kicked them right and left, and finally bayoneted or stabbed a colored resident of the city. Not an arrest was made for the stabbing. The authorities were cowed by the military.[12]

## PROGRESS OF STRAIGHT-OUTISM

The Fort Moultrie Centennial was not enough. The whites, with a few exceptions, continued quiet. Something more was needed. The leaders were at a loss what to do, when suddenly they met with the most unexpected resistance.

The fact is, many of the whites of this State, and prominent whites too, have had a hand in the rascalities of the State government. It is well known that not a few of them, knowing the Legislature to be corrupt, have used money to procure the passage of Bonanza bills, by which, through corporation speculations, they have been able to make immense gains. Others, more bold, have not scrupled to aid in plundering the treasury or otherwise cheating the Government. Now, among such deeds of spoliation was the Greenville and Columbia Railroad bond transaction, by which the State was swindled out of millions of dollars. Not far belated it was the Blue Ridge Railroad affair.[13] Originally carpet-bag schemes, they were joined in by a number of prominent white Democrats in the eastern and northeastern part of the State. Now it is needless to say that the perpetrators of these deeds have invariably fallen into bad repute among the main body of the whites. Eschewed and bitterly denounced, they saw, when the straight-out commotion began, a

*Gen. Martin W. Gary, considered by many the major architect of the Democrats' "straight-out" campaign of 1876. Photo courtesy of the South Caroliniana Library, University of South Carolina, Columbia.*

chance of regaining their lost influence. Accordingly, Greenville, where several of the peculators lived, was the birthplace and became the headquarters of straight-outism. That the peculators used their money freely to set the ball in motion is a fact well understood. But Edgefield County contained two leaders whose influence at home and in the white counties was so powerful as hardly to be depreciated by bonanza manipulation. Those men were Gens. M. C. Butler and M. W. Gary, aristocrats, fire-eaters and duelists. They were loud in advocating the straight-out movement.[14] They succeeded in putting in a henchman as editor of their only journal, a weekly in their county, and soon had the people of Edgefield on fire.[15] But out of Edgefield and the white counties their attorney actually impeded the advance of the idea. They were both candidates before the State Democratic Convention in the Spring for election to the National Convention at St. Louis and were both defeated. But they hoped on and played their cards well.

## RACE CONFLICTS—HAMBURG.

Race difficulties became frequent in Edgefield. At last, in June, six negroes accused of the murder of two whites were seized by an armed band of white men, evidently well organized, and shot. They were made to face the force, and every man at the word of command, emptied the contents of his gun into their bodies. The affair stirred up much bad blood between the races all over the State. The Republicans denounced it, and the Governor, though he knew it to be useless, offered a reward for the apprehension of the lynchers. The straight-outers and fire-eaters sided with the lynchers. But so pacified had the whites become under Chamberlain that many were found to condemn the shooting as cruel, unnecessary, and likely to produce trouble. This affair is known as the lynching of the Harmon murderers.[16]

Gen. Butler now resolved on a bold, desperate stroke. It was the massacre at Hamburg. Every one is familiar with that horrible tale.[17] I desire to call attention to the evident premeditation of the whole affair. A State militia company composed of negroes was parading on the Fourth of July. Two young aristocrats, one of them a Butler, drove up the street in a buggy, and instead of turning aside demanded that the militia should give way. After some ineffective protests this was done. They drove past. The captain was ere long indicted for obstructing the highway. The young men and the father of one of them were the prosecutors. Hardly had they reached the office of the justice when armed bands of white men began to pour into town; the captain and the company, all residents of the town, hastily assembled at their armory for consultation. The whites soon made a demand on them for their arms; unable to understand the right of a band of rioters to disarm a legal military company, and fearful of their treatment should they surrender, they refused. Fire was opened on them. They returned it after a half hour. Then hundreds of armed Georgians hurried over the bridge from Augusta, on the opposite side of the Savannah River, and joined in the contest. Finally a cannon was brought from Augusta and the company compelled to abandon the house. Many of them were captured. Of these, seven were shot in cold blood and the rest turned loose and fired on as they departed; and the rioters, after despoiling the property of their victims, broke up and departed for home. Butler was at the bottom of the conspiracy, which will go down in history with Glencoe and Wyoming, condemned to the eternal execration of humanity.[18]

## THE CONVENTION.

Butler had calculated well. The affair stirred up the passions of the races. The straight-out organs boldly defended it. Every fire-eater defended it. They caught at the chance. Country papers were purchased. Every county was canvassed. The passions of the Confederate soldiers were appealed to. The young men were called upon to rally to the support of Gen. M. C. Butler, who had lost a leg in the defense of South Carolina, and won honors in the war. The editor of The News and Courier had, as far as he dared, put the outrage in its true light. An attempt was made to throttle him. Gen. Gary strove to engage him in a duel. Mr. Rhett also tried to foist upon him an affair of honor.[19] Both were thwarted, but at the expense of much influence to the editor, as a withdrawal from a duel is still considered cowardly and degrading in South Carolina. The organization of Democratic clubs, rifle companies, and mounted companies was rapidly begun. The fire-eaters induced all the young men to join them, and send to Coventry those who would not.[20] The call on the President for troops by the Governor, although absolutely justified by Hamburg, was also used to stir up animosity. The State Democratic Convention was called unusually early by the Central Committee, composed largely of fire-eaters, and the election of delegate after delegate pledged to straight-outism in the compromise counties indicated the success of these tremendous efforts. The convention finally met on the 15th of August. The straight-outs were in the majority. But so strong was the confidence of the whites in Gov. Chamberlain that notwithstanding all the exertions that had been made, this majority was only a few votes. But it was sufficient. The convention resolved to nominate a straight-out Bourbon Democratic ticket, and to make a desperate attempt to carry the State on the Mississippi plan. The ticket was nominated. Every man on it is an ex-Confederate officer, and bears wounds received while fighting against the Union. And at the head of it, nominated for Governor, stands Wade Hampton, the aristocrat of the aristocrats, the fire-eater of the fire-eaters, a famous general in the Confederate army, the reincarnation of Calhounism, Jeff. Davisism, anti-Northism and Southern intolerance. After the measure was once resolved upon the delegates acted in concert. Butler, the hero of Hamburg, placed Hampton in nomination before the convention. The whites once more resolved to trust them and surrendered at discretion. The convention gave sentence for open war. After a torchlight procession and a mammoth ratification meeting the delegates went home with a full understanding of the methods to be employed.

## A MASS MEETING IN SOUTH CAROLINA.

And by St. Paul the work has gone on bravely. Never since the passage of the Ordinance of Secession have there been such scenes in the State. The whole white population is up in arms and drilling. Wade Hampton and his colleagues are canvassing the State. Everywhere they go there are mass meetings and torchlight and military processions, recalling those of 1860-61. A widespread system of terrorism and intimidation reigns supreme. The negroes, now so long unmolested that they have come to look upon freedom as the natural order of things, have been suddenly awakened from their dream. They see the military drilling all around them. Dark faces scowl at them when they go abroad. They hear of secret meetings and gatherings of their old-time owners. Whisperings of the Hamburg butchery reach them. They hear the whites all around them saying that the bottom rail has been on the top long enough—that the darkey has got to step down and out— that Hampton must be elected. In alarm they call a mass meeting of the Republicans for consultation. Their prominent men are invited to be present and speak. The time comes. Thousands are present. They organize and the speaking begins. Suddenly a commotion arises. The orator stops. The tap of the drum and sound of the bugle are heard down the road. Two long columns of white soldiery, armed to the teeth, mounted and on foot, come filing around the corner and march to the platform. They push aside the frightened negroes and select the best seats. Their leaders, ex-Confederate officers, then mount the platform and demand half the time for Democratic speakers. It is tremblingly accorded. A Confederate General arises, delivers a blood-and-thunder harangue, telling the negroes they have been fools long enough, have got to discard their present leaders and come back to their old masters, who intend to carry the election, peaceably if they can, but forcibly if they are resisted. A Republican follows. He is greeted with a storm of hisses and a deafening yell of derision from the military. He mutters a few words, every sentence being drowned by the hootings. At last a sentiment is uttered loud enough to be heard. Forthwith an armed bully storm[s] forward from the ranks and pronounces that assertion a lie. The speaker dares not resent the assault—nay, he dares not notice or allude to it. He talks on for a while. But the insults, jeers, impertinent questions, & c., come faster and faster, and finally, in alarm for his life, he resumes his seat. When the hissing has subsided, another Confederate takes the floor. He goes over the rambling remarks of the poor Republican, pronounces each and every one of them an infamous, malicious, damnable lie, and dares him to arise and say they are not. There is wild cheering. The Republican, quivering with fear and indignation, is forced to swallow it at the point of the bayonet. The other speakers on his side are treated in the same way. The meeting breaks up with three times three and a tiger for Hampton and Tilden. And such of the negroes as have not already fled in alarm are followed to their homes by the jeers and curses of the riflemen.

## VIOLENCE.

But this is not all. The air is filled with reports of outrages and murders which never appear in print. No prominent Republican of either color can safely leave town. Let a hint that he intends to ride out into the country get wind and he is sure to be ambushed. But more than this. The whites regard a Republican of their color with tenfold the vindictiveness with which they look upon the negro. Scores of white Republicans are hurrying in alarm to the newspaper offices to insert cards in which they renounce their party and profess conversion to Democracy. If these men hang back and refuse to neglect to join the precinct club or the nearest military company, their conduct is reported to the township meeting. A committee is appointed to request an explanation. They call on the suspected man at their earliest convenience. If he be sensible, he will submit profuse apologies and regrets, and hurriedly take up his rifle and follow them to the drill-room. Three or four white circuit judges have been dragooned into conformity, and the crowd of lesser lights threatens to absorb every white Republican in the State, except Gov. Chamberlain and the United States Senators.

There is no doubt of it that many white men and negroes have already been murdered in cold blood. In the Hamburg region, especially, the butchery of the blacks is wholesale. Even as I write there comes the account of another conflict at Ellenton, a few miles from that memorable spot.[21] And The Charleston News and Courier, now also dragooned into thorough conformity, after trying to insinuate that the negroes started the affair by heading its dispatch relating to the gathering of the rifle clubs with the words, "In arms in self-defense—a battle imminent," proceeds to add as minor headings the astounding words, "Two whites certainly killed; only 25 or 30 negroes killed so far." A stranger on casting his eye down the column and reading a vivid description of unprovoked attacks by mobs of negroes on the rifle clubs, cavalry companies, and sheriff's posse, in which the latter were taken altogether unawares, might have supposed that the printer was in error; that he should have said 25 whites killed and only two negroes; but, no; at the bottom of the article is a statement of the casualties, in which the same tell-tale information is given. And among the 25 or 30 "known to be killed' is a negro member of the Legislature.[22]

## "ONE MAN KILLED."

If a white man refuses to join the precinct clubs[;] if a white man's loyalty to the party is suspected; if a white Republican persists in his opinions, he is spotted, marked, doomed. He is scowled at if he walks abroad. If he passes a crowd of loitering whites at a street corner, an ominous silence falls on them till he is out of hearing. No warning be given him. No midnight visits are now paid or Ku-Klux missives dispatched. The whites have found by bitter experience that such things are boomerangs, which return with ten-fold force to injure the thrower. They manage the matter better now. They wait till an obnoxious man whom they have deemed as a victim chances to stand or pass near them, say on the public square, at the post-office, in a bar room, on the street. A crowd of white desperadoes will muster near him or follow him. They appear to be drunk, and begin to quarrel over some silly matter having nothing to do with politics. Several bystanders come up and take sides. Finally blows are exchanged, pistols drawn, and a regular free fight occurs. Shots are fired by all the party. Yet, strange to say, when order is restored, it is found that not one of the combatants is injured, while the poor Republican has been struck by several rounds of shots and killed. An account of the affray appears in the press (the press is almost wholly Democratic) under the heading, "Street Row—One Man Killed." Not only are single men picked off in this way, but sham fights are arranged by white ruffians on some non-political pretense, which swell to the proportion of riots, and in which several Republican bystanders are killed by chance shots, while some of the combatants are hurt. Of course the authors of these deeds go unpunished. In the first place, it is impossible to tell who fired the shot. Then it is unsafe for any one to indict anybody about it, or for the officials to be too zealous in investigating or prosecuting. But if an assassin does get into trouble by imprudence, his comrades, who of course compose most of the bystanders, are called as witnesses, and swear him out safely by giving in doctored testimony.

## PERJURY.

Yes, they will perjure themselves. The Democrats have resolved to stoop to any depths to conquer. And wholesale perjury is a part of their tactics. The press gives "cooked" accounts of everything—accounts "cooked" to suit Democratic palates, and not offend Northern sentiment, which they fear to do because they might lose Tilden votes in the North and draw down garrisons of United States troops on the State. For instance, with all their care, the leaders have not been able to prevent, occasionally, some undisguised political bloodshed. But though white cut-throats were the aggressors, the papers charged the aggression of the murdered Republicans. If a thing is too bad, then it is suppressed. In short, the local news of the Democratic journals of this State is just about as trustworthy as the official telegrams of the Servians and Turks.

The most atrocious instance of this perjury policy is to be found in the later history of the Hamburg affair. The ringleaders of that affair, finding from the debates in Congress and from Gov. Chamberlain's proceedings that their crime was likely to harm the Democratic cause North, assumed a tone of injured innocence. Those accused came forward, with a host of rowdies at their back to keep them in countenance, and surrendered to a Democratic judge. They then demanded to be bailed, and in support of this demand Gen. Gary, their counsel, brought forward a mass of affidavits, containing the most stupendous and barefaced perjury ever heard in a court-room since the days of Oates and Bedloe.[23] These affidavits made the negro militia the aggressors from the very start, charged them with delaying the buggy half an hour and insulting the young men grossly, justified the demand of the rioters for the arms of State militia, accused 25 frightened black wretches cooped up in a building by myriads of white desperadoes ravening for their blood with having opened fire and kept it up half an hour before it was returned, &c. These unparalleled falsehoods were early caught up by the Democratic press. At this day Gen. Butler and his troopers are pitied by thousands of honest people for the foul indignities they received, and for the outrageous attack made on them by throngs of black demons! It is a wonder that these exemplary witnesses have not gone on to relate how the immense crowd of infuriated demons succeeded in penning up the General and 25 of his men in a house; how they besieged it, dislodged the occupants, captured a large portion of them, and then cruelly and deliberately shot seven of the number! Mark how plain a tale shall put them down: The accounts of the holocausts first given to the world, and on which the popular conception of the affair is founded, were published in the Democratic journals of Charleston and Augusta—Charleston, the birth-place of secession, and Augusta, the home of Alexander H. Stephens. The damned spot will never out. All the perfumes of Arabia cannot sweeten the hands of the murderers.

## THE MISSISSIPPI PLAN.

I now find myself carried back to the time of secession. Then no Southerner dared avow Union sentiments. There were thousands of them in the South, but they were ruthlessly subjected to a system of terrorism, and had to choose between conformity and almost certain death; and with hardly an exception they conformed. To-day there are thousands of whites forced into this Confederate revival against their judgment and inclination; but they must conform or take the consequences. They conform, and then, to avoid the imputation of lukewarmness, they endeavor to prove their sincerity by outdoing their comrades in violence. The same men head this movement who led the State into secession. They have thoroughly revived the policy of intimidation. Talk of the blacks being intimidated! It is through the intimidation of the whites that the intimidation of the blacks is rendered possible. The election is to be carried on the Mississippi plan; and a part of that plan, be it remembered, was the intimidation of the whites. Wade Hampton is as much a Mississippian as a South Carolinian. It is true that he is descended from Carolinians famous in the Revolution, that his ancestors have always lived in this State, and that the family homestead is in the City of Columbia. But besides the immense estates he owned in South Carolina before the war, he had vast demesnes in Mississippi and other Southern States. This will not seem surprising when I mention the fact that he possessed 90,000 acres of land in fee simple, and owned 4,000 slaves. Now the war took from him the bulk of his property. But so much remained after all his losses that he is at this day the wealthiest man in the Southern States.[24] Most of his property now, however, is in Mississippi. He has abandoned by far the larger part of his ancestral estates in South Carolina. Though his home is in Columbia, he spends half his time on his plantations in Mississippi. He has one plantation there on which 800 of his former slaves are employed—so well has he been able to keep up this old plantation plan while the small farm system has been becoming well nigh universal. The fact I desire to call attention to is this: Hampton was in Mississippi prior to the last election there, which the Democrats carried by the shot-gun policy. The similarity of the methods employed by the Democrats in the canvass going on here now, with Hampton as their leader, forces me to the conclusion that the experiment is to be repeated here.

# A Southern Camp.
# Anarchy in South Carolina.

*(From a white native and resident of South Carolina who is not a Republican.)*
*New York Tribune*, October 16, 1876

The State To Supply the United South with Brains—The Broad Farce
of Making Democratic Proselytes among the Negroes—The Charleston
Riot—The Whites Sobered by the Violence of the Blacks—Intimidation of
Both Sides.

CHARLESTON, S.C., OCT. 10—The fire-eaters, I had hoped, would be improved by adversity. But, as I know too well from personal observation, they have borne within them a mind not to be changed by place or time. Like the Bourbons, they have returned to leadership, having learned nothing and forgotten nothing. They have entered into this campaign with the most criminal intentions. Their conduct reminds me of the remark of Moore that "the minds of some statesmen, like the pupil of the human eye, contract themselves the more the stronger light there is shed upon them."[1] Well may the Republican platform express apprehension at the prospect of a united South ruling the councils of the nation. The advent in Congress of Ben Hill and Proctor Knott has driven the old Bourbon element at the South into a species of insanity.[2] The palmy old ante-bellum days, they fancy, are about to return. "If we can't get out of the Union," they say, "why, then, we'll stay in the union and rule it. We'll elect Tilden and carry Congress again—both Houses. We shall then return to Washington and do as we used to do in the days of Calhoun and Buchanan. We'll dominate, socially and politically." Already they have entered a wedge, as the last session of Congress indicates; and now South Carolina and Louisiana are making every exertion to get their fingers in the pie. In South Carolina, I know, the desire of the leaders to do this is almost monomaniacal. "The present House of Representatives," say they, "is well enough, as compared with a Republican House. But though there is a Democratic majority in the body, and a majority of those Democrats are Southerners, there is one thing lacking: there are no leaders among them. They have no master minds to mark out policies, and devise bold expedients. Now it has always been the province of South Carolina to supply the Democracy with leaders. It has given them Calhoun, Preston, Lowndes, McDuffie, and Hayne.[3] "The Confederacy failed," says the fire-eater, "because South Carolina was not allowed to direct its councils—because Davis and not

Rhett was made President. The same is the case now: the Democracy need counselors and leaders, and of such we have an abundance to give them." Accordingly, the leaders of the South Carolina Democracy are crazed with the desire to go to Washington. Every tale of official corruption, every social scandal, is hailed with exultant cries of "You can't expect anything better of Yankees." The one desire of their souls, next to putting down the negro, is to go to Washington and turn things, politically and socially, upside down.

I ought to mention that their detestation of President Grant is absolutely without bounds. For Mr. Fish they have some respect, as he is of the old Knickerbocker stock. The same circumstance accounts largely for their enthusiasm for Gov. Tilden. They cry up Charles Francis Adams, too, for his wealth and ancestral distinction. For President they would have preferred Mr. Bayard, as being, if anything, a purer aristocrat than Gov. Tilden, besides having Southern prepossessions; but they judge Gov. Tilden to be the most available candidate—the best tub to fling to the Northern whale.[4] But though Gov. Tilden or Mr. Bayard will do for the present, things will never be straight, they think, till Southerners dominate both at the Capital and in the White House; for they devoutly believe that the blooded aristocracy of the old Southern plantations is superior to anything outside of the landed gentry of England. These things, indeed, are not expressed on the stump or in the papers. One hears them only in social intercourse, and no Northerner could hear them there. The Democrats have method in their madness. Their editors and orators are allowed to say nothing calculated to cost Mr. Tilden votes in the North. "We must be patient, we must wait, we must be prudent," say the papers and the speakers. They are afraid that there will be an explosion, that they will not be able to hold back the tiger long enough. They loudly assure the negroes that there is no design to keep them out of office, and then coolly ask them to vote the Democratic ticket. Well may Gov. Chamberlain sarcastically exclaim that their conversion to loyal sentiments is as sudden as that of Paul of Tarsus to Christianity.

### VI ET ARMIS.

Every result of the war is being deliberately undermined in South Carolina. I am aware of the repugnance with which the sending of troops to the South has come to be looked upon by the people of the North. The power has been unnecessarily exerted on some occasions—though if President Grant were in South Carolina to-day, he would undoubtedly be tempted to repeat with tenfold energy his assertion, that the Hamburg affair was a direct proof of the justification and necessity of his whole policy toward the reconstructed States. The Constitution undoubtedly gives the National Government authority to protect a State against domestic violence. Now that domestic violence exists in South Carolina is a fact as well ascertained, as probably and as absolutely certain as the commission of Turkish atrocities in Bulgaria. Otherwise what mean these facts: that 100,000 revolvers and Winchester and Remington breach-loading rifles have been imported into this State during the past two months; that a dozen batteries of artillery have been bought; that 75,000 whites, men and boys, are under arms—of whom 45,000 are trained veterans from the Confederate army, admirably equipped, organized not only in clubs, companies, battalions, and regiments, but with officers, who, from the sergeants, lieutenants, and captains up to the majors, colonels, and generals, have already long borne military titles obtained not by service in the militia, but on the fields of Manassas, Malvern Hill, and Gettysburg; that every Republican meeting is interfered with by armed regiments of soldiery, the speakers compelled to divide the time with Democratic orators, and then hooted down, browbeaten, made to swallow the lie, and threatened with violence; that in the Harmon, Hamburg, and Ellenton affrays, 45 negroes, according to the reports of State Democratic papers, have been killed in one section of the State, and that in the compass of a score of miles from the home of Gen. Butler, every white suspected of Republicanism is hastening to deny the charge and join the rifle clubs; that every white Republican, from Circuit Judges (three already out of eight) and State Attorneys down to private citizens, are hastening to renounce their principles and embrace Democracy to save their lives, though they dare not say so; that negroes and Republicans are being kicked right and left, jeered and scowled at, insulted, shot down in pretended street fights, and in every possible manner intimidated. What, I repeat, do all these things mean? How can violence be suppressed by the State Government? The colored militia is all it has to call upon, and if it calls upon this force, a bloody race conflict will be the result. The only resource is the United States Government. Military interference with Republican meetings should be peremptorily stopped. The polls should be carefully guarded on election day, and every Confederate company of soldiery found parading or lurking in the neighborhood forced to disperse. For here allow me to explain that the supreme effort of the Democrats is to be made on election day; 80,000 whites will be under arms, with their positions assigned. Companies will parade through every negro settlement to prevent them from leaving home to vote. Wherever it may be possible large cordons of soldiery will surround the polls and keep the Republicans from voting. The roads will be patrolled by squads of cavalry instructed to jeer at and bully every negro who is seen stirring from his house. If the whites succeed in getting into power as easily as in Mississippi, and then an attempt be made to reconstruct the State, there will be an explosion here which would instantly shake all the South as tremendous as that of 1860-61. The white leaders are aroused. "We have been suffering," say they, "for eight or ten years under a bondage worse than death. We intend to make a last desperate effort to redeem ourselves; and if the United States Government tries to put us back, why then we will not submit as Penn did in Louisiana, but the Government shall have to force us to obey, and we shall resist to the last man."[5] Such is the talk at every fireside, on every verandah, and at every street corner in South Carolina. I believe that the whites, if put down, will have to be kept under martial law. They will never submit to the negroes again even with a Chamberlain to control them.

## DEMOCRATIC CONVERTS AMONG THE NEGROES.

There has been much said of late about the intimidation by negroes of those of their race who wish to vote with the Democrats; and it has been asserted that large numbers of negroes have turned Democrats, despite this intimidation.[6] Now, when the canvass opened, if the State had been scraped with a fine-toothed comb, not a hundred colored Democrats would have been found within its borders—out of 95,000 colored voters. The white voters number 60,000 and a fraction. Therefore, they had to overcome a negro majority of 35,000. This they could only hope to do *vi et armis*, and through intimidation.[7] But if they were to do this undisguisedly they would injure Gov. Tilden's chances for the Presidency, and might be subjected to military correction. Their papers and speakers began from the start to appeal to the colored people to vote for Hampton. Then came accounts that negroes were beginning to join Democratic clubs. Then paragraphs descriptive of the great processions which have greeted Hampton and the other nominees as they have stumped the State. For instance: "A conspicuous feature of the procession was a column of 25 colored men, who have recently renounced Republican and become Democrats. They were enthusiastically cheered."

But unfortunately none of the spectators could ever find out who these proselytes were. At last hints of the truth began to leak out. Wade Hampton and his stumping party number about 20 men. Of these all assist in the speaking, taking turns about, though only about a third of them are candidates. Well, these gentlemen are making their circuit a real pleasure tour. Each of them is accompanied by his colored valet or waiting-man. Now these waiting-men are to a man Democratic—obsequious old family servants, who sneeze when their masters take snuff. So large is the party that two special cars have to be chartered on every railroad they go over. These colored waiting-men, cried up as recent converts in the papers, their numbers being swelled by a few local or imported colored Democrats. These waiting-men of Hampton and his merry company have furthermore been made to join every Democratic precinct club in the State where meetings were held while they were in town; and "twenty-five new converts" is triumphantly paraded at the head of the Charleston dailies the next day.

But negroes have been seen at local meetings and parades where Hampton and the waiting men were not present. These consist invariably of two or three colored Democrats really to be found in the neighborhood, while the rest are imported for the occasion from other places at a distance, their expenses being paid out of the treasuries of the parading clubs. On some occasions, unable to procure real Democrats, Republican negroes from a distance have been hired to come and form the column of converts; almost any of them will do it for a dollar a day and traveling expenses. I have been informed by a prominent Democrat that at one backwoods celebration where they failed through some reason to get any blacks at all to attend, the chairman of the Committee of Arrangements gave the one [dollar] to a party of young white men, who coolly rubbed their faces and hands with burnt cork, improvised wigs, took their places in the line with the utmost gravity, and played their parts undetected to the end. The papers, after chronicling a "new accession," will often add "this makes 65 colored men altogether who have joined the club." But a stranger attending one of these meetings would notice that the members begin to grin as soon as the secretary calls the roll of colored members, and he would hear only two or three responses to five or six dozen names. And, let him attend as often as he pleased, he would never see more than two or three negroes in the hall. The explanation is that the colored membership of the club is, on paper, 65, while the bona fide members are three in number.

## THE CHARLESTON RIOT.

But what about the Charleston riot?[8] Well, the fact is, the negroes do intimidate a man of their color who desires for any reason to turn Democrat. They will turn him out of their churches; none of the women will marry him, or talk with him[;] the men also ostracise him, and if he is caught where there are no white men, he is sure to be mobbed, stoned, and beaten. The negroes frown down and punish colored Democrats as sternly as the whites frown down and punish white Republicans; perhaps more sternly, though there is this to be said in their favor, that, while the whites intimidate both whites and colored Republicans, the negroes confine themselves to their own race, and leave the whites alone.

According to the Democratic papers the Charleston riot occurred as follows: A colored Democratic club had been organized in the city. The mass of the negroes thereupon became greatly excited. A large body of them besieged the hall of the club one night while its members were in session. Afraid of violence, they requested and procured a detail of 40 men from the white rifle clubs to escort them home. Guarded by these they marched out into the street. They then proceeded on their way, the mob following. After several members of the colored club had been dropped at their homes, the mob began to grow tumultuous. Finally they made a rush upon the procession. The white riflemen were over-powered by numbers and disarmed; several were shot, and one died the next day; and about half of them in company with the colored Democrats were clubbed. There was some firing by the riflemen, but it did not take effect. The mob, growing larger and larger, then surged excitedly up and down the main thoroughfares, shooting at or beating every white man who dared appear. For hours these infuriated rioters held possession of the city, spreading alarm and terror, and set the police at defiance. Such is the Democratic account.

The actual facts are these: As soon as Hampton was nominated the fire-eaters began their work of intimidation. A vast torchlight procession, during the course of which the negroes were about as unceremoniously ridden over as during the Fort Moultrie Centennial, opened the work. Rifle club after rifle club, and battery after battery of artillery was then organized. Arms were carried into the city. The drilling went on night and day. Then began armed interference with Republican meetings. Then came proposals in the papers and resolutions by the rifle clubs and Democratic meetings, to turn negroes out of employment if they persisted in voting the Republican ticket, and to employ Democratic colored laborers in preference to those who were Republicans. Hundreds of negroes were discharged on account of their politics. The Republican colored hackmen, draymen, and mechanics were soon unable to procure work, while a few who were Democrats were overcome by the press. Great excitement arose. The crowd on the streets grew larger and larger. Then came announcements that negroes were joining the Democratic clubs. This increased the excitement and bitterness. Finally it was announced that a Democratic club was to be formed composed exclusively of all the colored Democrats in the city. The time came. Ninety-seven negroes were enrolled. They were jeered by the blacks in the street as they left the hall. Frequent meetings of the club were held. It was the sensation of the city. Crowds of spectators attended its meetings. Confederate generals addressed them. Merchants and cotton factors went before them and publicly promised to employ all who would join it, even if forced to turn away workmen satisfactory in everything but politics. In this way several dozen converts were made. The hatred of the negroes daily threatened to break out in an explosion.

## A GAME TWO CAN PLAY AT.

In the midst of the excitement all the Republican primaries in the city met to nominate delegates to the State Convention of the party. Every colored man in the city turned out, and thousands of others came in from the outlying plantations and the Sea Islands close by, as spectators. The rifle clubs had concerted to break up these meetings, but so tremendous and so desperate were the throngs that the attempt was judged unwise and was abandoned. But a meeting of the colored Democratic Club was held that night. As the Republican primaries one by one adjourned, the crowds in the streets grew dense. Many Republican negroes dropped in to look on at the colored Democratic meeting. The speakers were full of abuse for the Republican primaries. Many of the negro listeners, full of indignation, went out into the street, and began to collect in groups and speak their minds. There was soon a large concourse. The [members of the] colored club, on adjourning, were afraid to come out, and procured an escort of white riflemen. As they filed out of the hall the crowd outside jeered. Some of the white riflemen retorted. Finally blows were exchanged as the excited mob pressed on; the combatants, at first only one or two, were at once joined by their friends, and finally some shots were fired—probably by both parties. At this the infuriated crowd rushed wildly on the riflemen and the colored Democrats, who were by this time in utter disorder. The negroes had few firearms, but most of them had sticks, as they are fond of carrying hickory canes. The whites and the colored Democrats were seized, beaten and knocked down. One man was killed and many were wounded and bruised. The papers stated that none of the rioters were hurt. But the riflemen nearly all fired once or twice, and must have done some damage. The negroes probably bore off their dead and wounded, knowing they had been doing wrong. After the whites and colored Democrats had succeeded in getting away, the mob, swollen to thousands, raged like wild beasts up and down the streets, attacking every white man who appeared, and keeping the city in terror all night. Nor did their fury subside for several days; but there was no outbreak, and peace was finally restored.

Since that time the city, then threatening to become the Vicksburg of the State, has been tranquil. The whites were terribly alarmed by that night's work.[9] They heard black demons raging up and down the streets before their houses, able to break in, rob, murder, and burn if they pleased. They found that, with all their organization, intimidation was a game two could play at, and that all the force was not on one side. The fear of fire has haunted them every since. The negroes might have fired the city that night. The interference with Republican meetings has come to an end. But the quiet is evidently that which precedes a tornado. The military organizations are kept up and new ones are forming. Artillery is pouring into the city. The whites are evidently preparing for a desperate attempt to get control of the polls on election day. That the conduct of the negro mob was outrageous is absolutely undeniable; but it is also undeniable that it was the logical sequence to the previous conduct of the whites. The negro (not standing very high anyhow biologically) is, when aroused, a wild beast. There is not the slightest doubt that in the use of the handy billy and the torch he is an expert of the first order; and it is probable that in the murder of women and children he can equal the Indian.

# The Political Condition of South Carolina

*The Atlantic Monthly* 39, no. 232 (February 1877)

---

*[The editors of The Atlantic Monthly have received from a South Carolina contributor the following paper, to the striking statements of which the fact that the writer is by birth, education, traditions, associations, and residence a Southerner ought to give additional value. Their interest in the present political juncture it is believed will amply justify the devotion of these pages to them. The writer's name is withheld for obvious reasons.]*

THE APPEARANCE OF THE NORTHERN ARMIES in the South during the late war was everywhere hailed with rejoicings by the negroes, and on the full achievement of their liberty through the defeat of the South their exultation was unbounded. The carpet-baggers came here in the army, in the service of the Freedmen's Bureau, and as agents of Northern churches and benevolent associations. They at once took the negro by the hand, and told him that the Northerners had freed him and intended to keep him free, give him property, and educate his children. The negro listened eagerly, and, well knowing his old masters were anything but satisfied with the new order of things, blindly followed the guidance of his new friends. Supplies were distributed, colored schools were founded, and the blacks were induced to leave the white churches and worship apart. Many colored men from the North, superior to their Southern brethren in culture, also came to help on the work.

A few of the carpet-baggers were pure men, zealots and philanthropists; but many were dishonest, adventurers who had left their country for their country's good. Reconstruction came. The enfranchised freedmen were utterly at sea in politics; they needed leaders. The Southern whites refused the opportunity, though it is doubtful if they could have secured it, with scorn. The carpet-baggers seized it. Their authority over the blacks was already assured, but to make it doubly sure the Union Leagues were established. Every negro joined them, and was awed by their mystic rites. Free political use was also made of the churches. The negro went to the polls, took a ballot from a carpet-bag friend, and without looking at it (with reason, for he could not read) dropped it in the box. He did not know what voting meant; he had only a vague though all-absorbing idea that it would bring him great good and avert great evil.

The constitutional convention of this State was held early in 1868. It was composed of carpet-baggers, scalawags (native white republicans), and a moiety of the brightest field-hands, ignorant of the alphabet. A constitution was framed—with a bill of rights prefixed which would have made Calhoun gasp and satisfied Jefferson and Sumner themselves—with clauses by which the State that originated nullification and secession is officiously made to declare that its citizens owe paramount allegiance to the constitution and government of the United States, and that the "State shall ever remain a member of the American Union; and all attempts from whatever source or upon whatever pretext, to dissolve the said Union shall be resisted with the whole power of the State."

The constitution was adopted and the first legislature and administration were chosen. The composition of the legislature was like that of the convention; the governor, attorney-general, and state treasurer were carpet-baggers; the lieutenant-governor and secretary of state were negroes; the house selected a scalawag for speaker.[1] Then began those fantastic tricks which for six years made the government of South Carolina the worst mockery of the name ever seen on earth. In the legislature no bills, unless of a purely legal character, could be passed without bribery, and by bribery any bill whatever could be passed. A formidable lobby sprang up, and presently organized depredations were commenced on the public; I will merely summarize the main performances. In the cases of the Greenville and Columbia Railroad and the Blue Ridge Railroad, the State had guaranteed railroad bonds to the extent of $6,000,000, reserving mortgages on the roads sufficient to cover the amount. Rings composed of carpet-baggers and native speculators paid the legislature to enact laws by which the State released her mortgages, still retaining her liability for the $6,000,000, and authorized the roads to pledge their property anew. In the case of the bank of the State, whose notes the State was bound to redeem, fraudulent notes to the amount of $750,000 were approved and assumed. The state-house was gorgeously fitted out; there were clocks at $480, mirrors at $750, and chandeliers at $650 apiece; elegant toilet sets were placed in the rooms of officials; there were two hundred fine porcelain spittoons at eight dollars apiece; and costly carpets, mirrors, sofas, etc., under the pretense of fitting up committee rooms, were furnished members for their apartments at boarding-houses. The real debt thus incurred was $50,000, but the contractor by sharing the spoil procured an appropriation of $95,000. Contingent funds became a notorious leak in the treasury; during the six years preceding 1875 they aggregated $376,000. During the same years the expenses incurred for the public printing ran up to the astounding figure of $1,104,000. During 1871, 1872, and 1873, they amounted to $900,000, or a thousand dollars a day.[2]

The bonded debt of the State, amounting to $5,800,000 when the new *régime* began, was run up to $27,900,000; and as the State was also liable for $6,000,000 of railroad debts, as above explained, its total debt was well-nigh $34,000,000. Most of the money raised on the bonds was deliberately stolen; and the legislature in 1873, alarmed by the clamor of the people and grudging the money paid for interest, repudiated about half the debt. The rate of taxation was almost incredibly heightened. Before the war the taxable value of property in the State was $490,000,000, and the taxes averaged $400,000 a year, the highest ever known being $515,678 in 1851. The valuation of taxable property since the war has been $184,000,000, and the annual taxes, state and county, have averaged $2,000,000! This is confiscation, pure and simple; and besides this the assessments have been outrageous. It is doubtful if the property assessed at $184,000,000 would bring $100,000,000 in market. Men were appointed auditors (assessors) whose figures would increase the amounts sent to the treasury to be stolen. I am personally familiar with seven or eight instances in which, owing to over-assessment, the tax amounted to five per cent of the real value of the property; and complaint on the subject was general. Municipal taxes, too, were extravagant. Such distress was engendered that at times half the real estate in the county would be advertised for sale for delinquent taxes.[3]

The officials in Columbia grew fabulously rich. Men, white and black, of no property went there, and, with no perceivable or conceivable means of honest living beyond a moderate official salary, would soon build palatial residences and support landaulets and blooded horses, worth more than their pay for a year. The state administration exceeded the legislature in corruption. They made stupendous over-issues when an issue of bonds was authorized, and pocketed the proceeds. In connection with the financial agency in New York, they perpetrated some of the boldest swindles that were undertaken. A commission had been appointed to buy $700,000 worth of lands to sell to freedmen, who met with difficulty at first in persuading their old owners to sell them land. This commission, by charging the State five or six times as much as they paid for lands, succeeded in stealing over a half million of dollars. The treasury was annually rifled of the taxes till it became bankrupt.[4]

The executive of South Carolina has unusual powers. With the approval of the senate he appoints the justices of the peace (called trial-justices here), county auditors, county treasurers, and many other local officers. The appointees for six years were corrupt whites, or equally corrupt and far more ignorant blacks, all rabid partisans. The colored justices could rarely read or write, and sent out their warrants signed with cross-marks. These officers were paid by fees, and were eager to listen to trivial complaints against whites, or to stir up litigation. The treasurers of the counties were often in default; and as they owed their appointment generally to the state senator from their county, they were compelled to supply him with the public funds whenever he called for them. The local officers elected by the people were on a par with the appointees of the governor.

To make matters worse, the fountains of justice were corrupted. The supreme court was composed of one carpet-bagger, one scalawag, and one negro.[5] The circuit courts, however, were not degraded. There were only two or three white or colored republicans competent to exercise judicial functions; and the whites, it was well understood, would not allow a perversion of power in this direction. So native white lawyers were generally selected for circuit judges—men who, retaining their honesty, would consent to keep quiet on politics, or openly profess republicanism. But to offset this there were juries composed chiefly of illiterate and degraded negroes, who thought their only duty was to find no bill or not guilty in all cases of blacks prosecuted by whites. Negro felons sent to the penitentiary were pardoned out by the wholesale. The highest number of prisoners in the penitentiary at Columbia (our only state prison) at any one time since the war has been four hundred and eighty. Yet in 1870 two hundred and five convicts there confined were pardoned. Pardons were granted as freely to men sentenced to serve for life or a term of years as to felons of a less degree of guilt. Negro convicts were generally pardoned, for political purposes, but money could obtain pardons for undeserving whites.[6]

The demoralization became inconceivable. Larceny was universal. If a man hung up his coat at one end of a field, before he could plow to the other end and back it was stolen. Cows turned loose to browse came home milked dry. Live stock of all kinds was killed in the woods in the day-time. Cotton was picked from the fields at night, and corn "slip-shucked." Gardens and orchards were stripped, and water-melons actually became a rarity on white men's tables. Burglary, especially of smokehouses and barns, was common. Everybody had dogs and guns, and thousands kept watch at night over their property.

In short, from 1868 to 1874 inclusive, the government of South Carolina was a grand carnival of crime and debauchery. After a year or so, the oppression grew so grinding that in many counties Ku-Klux Klans were organized. But their excesses soon carried the score over on the other side, and drew down the just indignation of the national government. They existed chiefly in counties where the whites outnumbered the negroes, and which had escaped the ravages of the war.

All these matters were aggravated by the management of the state militia. The militia officers appointed by the governors were all blacks, and the negro population eagerly enlisted. The whites scornfully refused to enlist under colored officers. The governor had power to receive any organization of private individuals, as part of the militia; but if he refused them, it was made highly penal to continue the organization. In several places the whites formed companies of their own, and offered themselves to the governor, who invariably refused them, and caused them to disband; but for the negro militia, one thousand Winchester and nineteen thousand Springfield rifles, with plenty of ammunition, were purchased. Armed with these, they drilled in a manner highly insulting and alarming to the whites. The military companies were used to tickle the negro's taste for martial pomp, and keep the negro vote consolidated.

## IT IS NOW TIME TO CONTEMPLATE THE OTHER SIDE OF THE PICTURE.

For years after the fall of the Confederacy the people could not hear a renewal of war mentioned without a shudder. Politics fell into abhorrence. The leaders of secession lost their influence. We had been told that the Yankees would back up against the North Pole before they would fight; that one man could drink all the blood which would be shed. But the North had warred promptly, aggressively, and successfully, and rivers of blood had run; consequently, the commands of the North were obeyed, the ordinance of secession was repealed, the constitutional amendment abolishing slavery was ratified, reconstruction was not resisted. The old leaders, indeed, were not disposed to submit. They bitterly protested against the enfranchisement of the freedmen, railed at the military government and the constitutional convention, tried to stir up enthusiasm for Seymour and Blair and a white-line democratic state ticket in 1868, and in every manner to rouse up the people; but their exertions were but ill-seconded.[7] There were state conventions of the democracy, indeed; but it is a remarkable fact that, for nearly eleven years after the war, there were, except here and there, no democratic primaries—precinct clubs—in South Carolina. Efforts were repeatedly made to form them, but the people would not join them, or, having joined, attend. It became the custom to elect delegates to the state conventions by calling mass-meetings of the county democracy at the county courthouse. These meetings elected the delegates, or made county nominations. Their only attendants, generally, were ten or a dozen gentlemen who had been our statesmen before the war.

The people regretted their defeat, and looked with hostility on both the emancipation and the enfranchisement of their slaves. The war and its results had cost them blood, property, and liberty; "But," said they, "it's no use trying to resist the current; the North is too strong for us, and is bound to have its way." To the solicitations of their more sanguine leaders they replied, "You have misled us once; we will be more prudent in the future." The course of President Johnson inspired them with hopes, but these fled when the unity of the North was perceived. The prospect of electing Seymour animated them to some extent, but events soon chilled them again. For years, voting was regarded as a mournful and onerous farce, and thousands refrained from it.

Even the new *régime*, with all its horrors, was submitted to, the sporadic out-breaks of the Ku-Klux forming the one exception. The leaders tried a change of tactics. In 1870 they dubbed the state democracy the Citizens' Reform Party, and, in the hope of catching part of the negro vote, nominated a Northern-born republican resident for governor, who accepted because dissatisfied with the party corruption.[8] They hoped through success to make a step towards regaining power. But the negroes remained solid, and the regular republican ticket was again elected. The leaders of the whites now acquiesced in the do-nothing policy. For four years the whites kept almost altogether out of politics. The nomination of Greeley, indeed, excited their hopes powerfully at first, but his election was soon perceived to be impossible.[9] No state ticket was run in 1872. There were two republican tickets in the field: the regular nominees supported by the corrupt element—and consequently the bulk— of the party, and a bolting ticket supported by some republican leaders, with their followers, who were in favor of reform. The few whites who turned out to vote for Greeley also voted for the bolting candidates, who, however, were defeated. The tax-paying democrats met once or twice after this to consult over their grievances, but confined themselves to temperate remonstrances, petitions, and non-partisan investigations.

In the election of 1874 there was again a split among the republicans. The party convention nominated a ticket at the head of which was Mr. Daniel H. Chamberlain, for governor.[10] He was supposed to be corrupt, as he had been attorney-general and a member of various important commissions at the time when corruption was greatest. The honest element again bolted. The whites met in convention, and resolved to support the bolting ticket. In return the bolters divided many local nominations with the democrats. The whites almost to a man voted for the bolting candidates,—county, legislative, and state,—although many of them (even the nominee for lieutenant-governor) were colored; so desperate at last had they become under governmental oppression. Mr. Chamberlain and the other regular candidates for state officers were elected; but the bolters and democrats elected about two fifths of the legislature.

The whites now expected the oppression to be redoubled. But when Mr. Chamberlain was installed, a curious spectacle was presented. He had made the usual promises of reform on the stump, amidst the smiles of his supporters, who had nominated him because they thought him a congenial spirit. He now announced that he had spoken in earnest. He made wholesale removals of the corrupt officers appointed by his predecessors, and replaced them by honest and competent men, in large part democrats. The corrupt schemes of the legislature were relentlessly vetoed. It was as bad as any preceding body, and elected two infamous men as circuit judges.[11] Terrible excitement arose, which the governor quieted by refusing to commission the judges on a legal quibble; and by his threatening to veto the usual extortionate tax-bill, the most reasonable one known since 1867 was procured. The corrupt regular republicans went into vehement opposition to the governor, while the bolters and the democrats rallied to sustain his vetoes.

The reforms in justice, however, were most widely, deeply, and immediately felt. The wholesale pardoning at once stopped; the penitentiary began to fill up; good jury commissioners (the executive names them), who would select decent blacks for jurors and give the whites half the panels, were appointed. The whites began to take interest in the courts, and to look with less disfavor on colored jurors; the corrupt justices walked the plank by scores; a great decrease of crime was perceptible in a few months; race hatred greatly subsided. It is impossible to express the immense feeling of relief experienced at the restoration of confidence in the government.

The whites were unable to make too much of their savior. He was admitted into the most aristocratic society. He was elected orator by the colleges, called on by fashionable associations to respond to toasts, and lionized everywhere. The white leaders and the papers called loudly for his reëlection, and though the corrupt element of his party were determined to nominate another man or bolt should he carry the convention, a large section was in favor of re-nominating him. The whites shuddered at the terrible ordeal they had gone through, and seemed ready to recognize the rights of the negro and do anything in the way of compromise to avert such evil in the future. In several municipal elections (noticeably in Charleston) mixed tickets, half democrat and half blacks or republicans, were elected. It seemed as if a political millennium were about to dawn.

The motives of the governor have been variously construed. The belief became common that he was a pure man and had been slandered in the past. Many, however, believed him to be talented, ambitious, and unscrupulous; declaring that he had been a corruptionist while it suited his designs, but that on becoming governor he had determined to turn over to the whites, get socially recognized, procure an election to the United States Senate, and go there with such a powerful Southern support behind him that he could play an important part in national politics. This is the belief of the whites at present. Governor Chamberlain is a cold, elegant man, a graduate of Yale, and a lawyer. He is a student of comparative literature, and is thoroughly familiar with the course of modern thought. Some cultivated men in the State say that he went with the current till he gained power to control it; that then, out of pure love of political science, he undertook to bring about a reconciliation between the races and solve the great problem of Southern reconstruction and harmony. That he has ambition they do not deny; but they look on it as the ambition of a statesman, not of a politician. They recall the cold, judge-like neutrality with which he presided over the people. He did not truckle to the whites, as he has been charged. He associated with them professedly as a republican, but avoided insulting their prejudices. He always gave the blacks strict justice. In his appointments he preferred republicans, when fit ones could be found; but where none were fit, he would select democrats.

The governor of South Carolina is elected every two years. Mr. Chamberlain was elected in November, 1874, simultaneously with the democratic national House of Representatives. The election of that house was hailed with thanksgiving in South Carolina, as an indication that the North had determined to protest against the oppression of the Southern whites by their old slaves and carpet-baggers. But, after a time, the fact began to attract attention that a majority of the democratic congressmen were Southerners, and many of those Southerners ex-Confederate generals. A wild hope seized our old political leaders that the palmy *ante-bellum* times were about to return, that the democracy was again to control the national government, and that the South was again to rule the councils of the democracy. Every Southern State was now democratic except South Carolina and Louisiana, and Louisiana was on the verge of a change. Even Mississippi, than which only South Carolina was worse Africanized, had been carried by the white-liners. Good government, indeed, was now restored in our State and by their assistance could be maintained. But it was not a government under their own auspices, or those of the democratic party; and while it continued they could hope neither to be heard at Washington nor to practice their cherished traditions at home.

From the beginning of 1876 they set themselves to the task of arousing the people. A violent cry was raised against the governor, and the whites were called on to follow the example of their brethren in the other Southern States. Social pressure was brought to bear, an energetic canvass begun, and newspapers were bought up or new ones founded; for the main body of the whites were still disposed to hesitate. "We had better wait," said they, "and see how things go in the North. If the democrats carry the elections there in November, and get control of the national government, why, of course, we can rise up and throw off republican rule in the State. But we have a good government now, and had best let well-enough alone, for fear our old oppression might be re-established." But the work went on. At the Fort Moultrie centennial thousands of Confederate soldiers, once more under arms, were paraded before the people of the State.[12] Wade Hampton was their captain. Hot Southern speeches were made, and the troops in attendance from Georgia, disgusted at the unwonted spectacle of negroes in office, rode rough-shod over the colored police of Charleston. Mr. Tilden had just been nominated at St. Louis, and the brilliant prospects of electing him were triumphantly paraded.[13] Then came race conflicts; the killing of a colored legislator in Darlington County, the lynching of two negroes in Marlboro and six in Edgefield, and finally the Hamburg massacre.[14] This last and the governor's action concerning it were followed by appeals to the whites, made with all the old vehemence of Carolinians. Everybody was urged to buy arms; rifle clubs and mounted companies were everywhere formed, the young men being cheered on to join them; and the old system of browbeating and challenging all non-conformists to the duello was vigorously put in operation.

The whites in the old Ku-Klux counties, where the negroes are in the minority, turned over *en masse* to the revolutionary policy; in the other counties they held back for a long time, discouraging violence as inexpedient, as likely to hurt Tilden in the North, as being, in short, *premature*. But gradually they half fell, were half driven, into line; though not all; for when the state democratic convention met on August 15th there was still a powerful minority (about two fifths) in favor of postponing action until it should be seen what the republicans would do about Chamberlain. It is useless to say, however, that the majority carried their point. General Wade Hampton, the Murat of the Confederacy, in whom are strikingly crystallized all the arrogant old plantation qualities of the South, was nominated for governor with a corresponding ticket.[15] It was determined to carry the State by the method known as the Mississippi Plan.[16]

I will merely summarize the means used; I was in the State during the whole campaign, and know whereof I speak. The plan was, first, to arouse the white population to secession or nullification madness; next, to get as many negroes as possible to vote the democratic ticket, and prevent as many as possible from voting the republican; and finally to put such a face on their doings as to work no harm to the democratic cause outside the State.

In the first matter they thoroughly succeeded. General Hampton,

*Wade Hampton III, Confederate general, South Carolina governor 1876-78, and later U.S. senator. Photo courtesy of the South Caroliniana Library, University of South Carolina, Columbia.*

an orator of no mean order, an accomplished gentleman sprung from the best Carolina stock, our greatest and most celebrated soldier, in company with numerous other ex-Confederate generals and officers (among whom were some from other States, including Toombs, Hill, and Gordon), began a systematic canvass of the State, speaking at every county town and at other places of size.[17] Such delirium as they aroused can be paralleled only by itself even in this delirious State. Their whole tour was a vast triumphal procession; at every depot they were received by a tremendous concourse of citizens and escorts of cavalry. Their meetings drew the whole white population, male and female (for the ladies turned out by tens of thousands to greet and listen to the heroic Hampton), for scores of miles around, and had to be held invariably in the open air. They were preceded by processions of the rifle clubs, mounted and on foot, miles in length, marching amidst the strains of music and the booming of cannon; at night there were torch-light processions equally imposing. The speakers aroused in thousands the memories of old, and called on their hearers to redeem the grand old State and restore it to its ancient place of honor in the republic. The wildest cheering followed. The enthusiasm, as Confederate veterans pressed forward to wring their general's hand was indescribable. Large columns of mounted men escorted the canvassers from place to place while off the railroad. They were entertained at the houses of leading citizens, held receptions attended by all the wealth, intelligence, and brilliance of the community, and used all the vast social power they possessed to help on the work.

Besides this, the fearful memories of the ante-Chamberlain days were revived. The governor's participation in them was maliciously asserted. The acknowledged fact that the mass of the negroes had opposed his reforms was skillfully paraded. His attempts to secure United States troops were denounced as a damning outrage; "South Carolina should be ruled by South

Carolinians" was repeated from mountain to sea-board.

The work of buying arms and organizing democratic primaries and rifle clubs was energetically pushed on, till every democrat in the State had a gun and was enrolled in a primary, and three fourths of the whites belonged to the military. The ostracism and dragooning of all who hung back was carried to the last extreme, until the whites were as consolidated as in 1860.

The negroes saw these portentous movements; they saw the soldiery drilling, and every white man spending hours daily at the target. Rumors of Hamburg reached them. Their former masters urgently importuned them to vote for Hampton. Every republican meeting was interrupted by armed multitudes of democrats, half the time demanded for democratic speakers, the republican orators jeered at, interrupted, vilely insulted, and hissed down, while the intruding speakers plainly announced that the whites were going to carry the election at all hazards and that the negroes had better vote the democratic ticket to save themselves trouble. Long lines of cavalry were kept constantly parading and proved particularly effective. Then another holocaust took place at Ellenton, and was talked about by the whites all over the State in the presence of the negroes.[18] The whites, furthermore, suddenly assumed a dictatorial demeanor in their daily intercourse with the colored people, knocked them down or shot them on the slightest provocation, and by free use of menaces prevented indictments. Prominent republicans, white and colored, were threatened with ambuscades or followed by crowds of bullies if they left towns to canvass in the country; the negroes and white republicans were insulted on the streets; if troublesome, they were forced into fights by bravoes or picked off by "chance" shots during the course of pretended drunken rows got up near them. Terrorism soon reigned supreme.

To conceal these things systematic deception was used. Hundreds of false affidavits were procured, charging the negroes with aggression at both Hamburg and Ellenton, and justifying the whites in everything, even in the murder of prisoners; the responsibility for every deed of democratic violence was fixed on republicans; reconciliation to the results of the war was loudly professed. For over a month hardly any negroes turned democrats, yet large accessions were triumphantly claimed in the papers; ten colored democrats were nominated for the legislature in counties sure to go republican; the negro majority, which the last census gives as thirty-five thousand (seventy-five thousand white voters and one hundred and ten thousand colored), was boldly asserted to be only ten or fifteen thousand; and the judges (mostly democratic whites who had professed republicanism, or consented to preserve silence) were induced to declare for Hampton and *Hayes* (the latter for effect North), and denounce Chamberlain; *though a few months before, each and every one of them had been the very loudest supporters he had in the State.*

So few colored men joined the democratic clubs during the earlier weeks of the campaign that, to make the matter sure, there came proposals in the press and resolutions by the precinct and rifle clubs to employ no colored republicans as laborers, and to give no patronage to republican brick-layers, blacksmiths, carpenters, hack-men, market-men, etc., when democratic negroes were accessible. Thousands of republicans at once had ruin of democracy staring them in the face as alternatives; and hundreds of them finally began to turn.

For election day a *coup d'état* was contemplated. The members of the rifle clubs informally agreed among themselves to guard the polls and systematically patrol the public roads in a menacing manner, so as to frighten off the negroes and keep them at home.

But suddenly the governor came out with his proclamation. In the earlier part of his administration he had accepted ten or a dozen rifle clubs as militia; but the hundreds that had been organized since the opening of the campaign had asked no permission and were clearly illegal. So he ordered them to disband, and (as commander-in-chief) he disbanded those he had accepted, they too having been turned into political machines. The papers announced a day or two beforehand that the order was to be issued; and added, falsely and maliciously, that the arms of the clubs would also be demanded, although private property, each member having purchased his own gun. It would have taken but a wave of Hampton's hand to cause a frightful outbreak; but he counseled submission, especially when the president's proclamation came out, as the more expedient course, and the clubs ceased drilling and parading, though, of course, retaining their arms; it would have taken but a drum beat to make most of them fall into ranks. Then United States troops were poured into the State, and a garrison was stationed at every important town. The interference with republican meetings was immediately stopped.[19]

When the democrats first began their demonstrations the negroes were cowed all over the State. They kept remarkably quiet, and it seemed as if their old fear of their masters would so reassert itself as soon to force them into the democratic ranks. But after a while in some of the counties where they predominate—noticeably Charleston, Darlington, and Orangeburg—they became intensely excited at what they judged this evident blow at their liberty. They purchased guns and ammunition as fast as they were able, burnished the arms the State had given them, had broken or rusty weapons repaired, got knives, clubs, and torches ready, consulted together secretly, and evinced a stern determination to resist aggression to the death. They furthermore, alarmed at the daily defections from their ranks on account of work taken from republicans, began in the most fearful manner to maltreat and intimidate every colored man who gave promise of turning democrat. The excitement over this matter in Charleston resulted in a terrible riot, during which the city for one night and practically for several days was in the hands of black savages, who shot or beat every white who appeared on the streets.[20] Indignant at the breaking up of their meetings by democratic soldiery, they began to attend armed. The bloody collision at Cainhoys was the consequence of this policy.[21] After the arrival of the garrisons, the negroes all over the State broke out into extravagant expressions of joy and thanksgiving, appeared under arms on every occasion, and acted in the most alarming manner everywhere. Their orators advised them to cut the throats of white women and children, if the shotgun policy were continued, and to apply the torch to the dwelling of any man who discharged them on account of politics. In a week or two the increase of crime was positively appalling. The whites had conjured up a spirit which threatened to tear them in pieces.

The republican convention met on the 12th of September. Governor Chamberlain used all his official power and personal influence to pack it with his adherents and the honest element of the party; but the corrupt element was in the majority. The governor was a candidate for renomination, and he urged as candidates for the other high offices men of acknowledged integrity and uprightness. But so bitterly had the corruptionist come to hate him that they made a violent onslaught on him; and although they knew that without his interference the whites would out-Mississippi Mississippi in the election, they gave him plainly to understand that they must no longer be trodden on by him. That it was necessary to success to renominate him they bitterly admitted; but beyond this they resolutely refused to go. The governor had either to stoop, or to turn over the State to the strongest and fiercest spirits of the section which had tried to tear the Union asunder. A compromise was effected [*sic*], and the governor was renominated; a few of the highest offices were given to his adherents, and the rest were given to the corruptest men in the corrupt section of the party. It was a sorry ticket; but, thanks to his efforts, it was the best put forward by the party convention since reconstruction. Similar compromises in the nominations were effected [*sic*] afterwards in many localities; but in a majority of counties the corruptionists broke out in open rebellion, put up their own men, and refused to give the Chamberlainites a showing; and the Chamberlainites and Mr. Chamberlain acquiesced.

The coming of the troops was a terrible backset for the democrats; but they had gone too far to recede. The troops were loudly welcomed, and their gentlemanly West Point officers entertained at formal but polite dinners to keep up appearances; although the furious deportment of the negroes soon made the whites, now unorganized, *really* glad that the troops were among them to prevent overt violence. A day of prayer and fasting for democratic success was appointed by the central committee of the party, and, at their request, religious services with the same object (an unknown thing) were held in every church—even Episcopal and Catholic—in the State. The "preference policy" was sternly pursued. Thousands of colored republicans lost their situations. Negro tenants (republican) were everywhere warned to leave. On trying to rent new lands they were coldly asked, "Are you going to vote for Hampton?" Republican craftsmen were everywhere idle. The papers and orators unintermittingly declared that every democrat should make it his duty to secure at least one negro to vote for Hampton, by fair means or foul, and watch him deposit his ballot. This was the famous "one man apiece" policy. In consequence, all the whites, especially gentlemen of property[,] emulated each other in purchasing voters. Thousands of negroes had liens on their crops released, land rented them at nothing, supplies promised for next year, or money paid them outright in consideration of their turning democrats, or of staying away from the polls. In consequence of the discharge of colored laborers, the torch began its terrible work all over the country, and the whites were compelled to keep watch over their property at night. The streets of every village were patrolled. All the more bravely did the whites face the torch, all the more zealously did they work, after the significance of the democratic victory in Indiana began to appear.[22] It was well known that the republican party there had made the issue on the "bloody shirt" and the "solid South," and on that issue had been defeated. Grant was furiously denounced from one end of the State to the other, and the people loudly called on to aid in electing a democratic president who would keep his hands off the South in the future. And the leaders, thinking everything was going for Tilden and the democrats, became absolutely frantic with the desire, which had been strong enough before, to participate in the victory, to get back to Washington, and to restore Palmetto ascendency in the national councils.

As the election day approached, there were signs that the republicans, frightened at the immense depletion of their strength, would attempt performances in repeating unparalleled in the history of elections;[23] and the democrats began on all sides to say that if the republicans tried that game the democrats should try it too. The rowdies and fire-eaters among the lower classes of whites were worked up with the notion, and made ready for anything.

The election passed off amid terrible excitement, but, on the whole, peaceably. United States troops were posted at a large proportion of the polls and places where trouble or overt intimidation was apprehended, and were called on frequently to repress incipient tumults. Both parties turned out in full force, and stayed at the polls all day. Guns were brought by both parties, and concealed in houses near many polls, but the troops would not allow any to be shown. The whites, though, to a man, wore pistols as usual, as did all the negroes, few in number, who had been able to buy them. In Barnwell County, however, the ballot-box at a rural poll in a negro section, where no troops were posted, was fired on by an unknown party (supposed of course to be whites) from a neighboring swamp, and a stampede occurred. The poll was closed. Afterwards the managers reopened it in an adjoining place, and the negroes were rallied, inspired with mob courage, and deposited 2027 votes. The democrats afterwards protested against the counting of these votes. In Charleston County the colored militia turned out at rural polls under arms, stood on guard near such as had no troops near them, and prevented scores of colored democrats from voting, or intimidated them into "voting right."

The election itself was one of the grandest farces ever seen. In counties where the negroes had terrorized affairs, streams of colored republicans poured from poll to poll all day, voting everywhere. The largest vote ever cast before in Charleston County had been twenty thousand. Yet on election day, although three or four thousand negroes were bribed or led by fear of starvation to refrain from voting, and although five or six hundred who did vote cast the democratic ticket, the total vote thrown reached the amazing figure of 23,891 and the county went republican by 6391 votes—six thousand having been the average majority in the past. In counties terrorized by the whites, white bravoes rode from poll to poll, and voted time and again. Hundreds of Georgians and North Carolinians crossed the borders and joined in the work. In Edgefield County the influx of Georgians and the repeating were simply tremendous. The total number of voters in that county, according to the recent state census (*which was denounced as exaggerating the population by the democratic press*, because the census takers were paid by a fee of five cents for every name recorded instead of by a salary), is 7122, and the county has always, hitherto, gone republican by one thousand votes; yet, although a thousand negroes certainly, and an unknown number above that, were induced by money or fear of starvation to refrain from voting, the total number of votes cast was 9289, and the democrats carried the county by the astounding and tell-tale majority of 3225![24] Similarly startling in most of the counties were the changes as compared with the census or past elections. Every democrat with whom I have talked since election day has something of this sort to say: "Why, the negroes at my precinct repeated and voted their minors on a tremendous scale; for their total vote was almost as high as ever before, although we kept away fifty or sixty from voting and got about a dozen to vote with us. Why, I carried one negro to the polls myself, and saw him put in his ballot all right, and his two brothers stayed at home all day, for I told them if they voted against us I would turn them off."

The ballots were undoubtedly counted fairly at the polls. Through Governor Chamberlain's influence, one democrat and two republicans had been appointed managers at every precinct. The board of county canvassers, appointed to aggregate the returns for each county, was similarly composed. But in compiling the vote they made some changes of the precinct returns; for instance, the names of some candidates of each party had been misspelt on the tickets by country printers, and in several cases candidates running for certain offices had by mistake received votes for other offices. The precinct managers returned the votes cast, but the county boards credited the candidates really intended to be voted for with the erroneous votes. The returns were awaited amidst the most intense excitement. They were exceedingly close, but at last it became apparent that, according to the precinct returns (excluding the Barnwell box where the voting was interrupted), the democratic ticket was ahead. But presently it was ascertained that the returns of the board of county canvassers would put the result in doubt, and that if the Barnwell box were received the republican ticket would prevail. This caused wild excitement, for the board of state canvassers, composed of the secretary of state, attorney-general, state treasurer, etc., has power to decide when there are variations in the returns, as well as to determine contested elections; and, of course, the republicans contested Edgefield and Barnwell—the latter, because the democrats had carried the county through the exclusion of the votes at the poll, so often referred to by the county canvassers—as well as Laurens County, where foul play was alleged. The whites had had great distrust of the state board from the start, for it had been a corrupt body always, and at present is not above suspicion, besides the fact of all its members being republicans and half of them candidates for reëlection.

When the board met, democratic counsel appeared before it, and, though the above-named powers were undoubtedly conferred on it by law, and had been exercised without question for eight years, the board's authority under the law to hear contests was objected to, the constitutionality of the laws constituting it were objected to, the right of the members to sit was objected to, and, in short, everything was objected to on contemptible quibbles (though it must be owned that the man who drew up our election laws might have made them clearer). Finally the board was dragged before the notorious supreme court. The chief-justice is F. J. Moses, Sen., father of the world-famous Robber-Governor who preceded Governor Chamberlain, and who was one of the corrupt pair whom Chamberlain refused to commission as judges. Father and son are alike inimical to Chamberlain.[25]

I can safely predict one thing: if the ultimate decision be in favor of the republicans, we shall have in South Carolina all the transactions so common in Louisiana—rival governors and legislatures, Penn insurrections and Wiltz *coup d'états*;[26] the democrats are aroused to the last degree, and with difficulty can be held in by their leaders, who are, of course, diplomatic. In the mean while, there is almost a reign of anarchy; the negroes are burning and stealing, the whites are shooting and beating; the papers are filled with reports of crimes and affrays. The races here are so worked up that anything may cause a bloody conflict; the whites could probably defeat the negroes easily, and slaughter them like dogs, but—the torch! The negroes would fire Charleston in a thousand places if driven to bay; the whites know this and restrain the young men; the negroes know it too, and are accordingly insolent and malevolent.

If Chamberlain be installed, he will undoubtedly try to do right; and as the legislature will have its lower house democratic or republican by a few votes only (if the democrats in the latter case will sit), with his aid good government is possible; but it is improbable, for the democrats are now in the mood to rule or ruin, and are likely to refuse to have anything to do with a government of republicans.

The popular terms, "the North" and "the South," the "Confederacy" and the "Union," are, as usual, descriptive of an underlying truth. There is and always has been a difference in national characteristics between the inhabitants of the old free, and those of the old slave States. The Southerners used to look on the Northerners as coarse, money-getting people, given to fanaticism on certain social, political, and religious questions. Their contempt for the commercial character of the North originated, of course, in the aristocratic training of the plantations, and their hatred for the liberty and equality doctrines of Northern philanthropists arose from the intolerance natural to all aristocracies, and from the dread of a servile insurrection or of losing their slave property. There was, undeniably, much antipathy felt by the people of the South towards the Northerners before the war. Now the war has not diminished, it has intensified this antipathy; the chivalric South, which had borne itself so haughtily and boisterously in Washington, was conquered by the commercial North; the doctrines of the fanatics were triumphant; cherished institutions were revolutionized. The master was made slave, and the slave made master. The hatred of the humiliated Southern people was absolutely unfathomable; and it yet continues. The talk about the healing of the recent wounds, the filling up of the bloody chasm, the reconciliation of the sections, etc., is opposed to common sense, reason, and the experience of ages, and the facts in the case. The South is a conquered land, and the Southerners, still retaining their disgust for the commercial and equalizing spirit of the North, have had national hatred added to national antipathy by their defeat. They have been quiet and submissive since the war, through pure exhaustion and animal fear, but ostracism of Northerners has been universal, and intermarriage is forbidden on the pain of social death. Sometimes, it is true, Northern settlers of unimpeachable antecedents, men of tact, who would keep out of politics and set themselves to the task of conciliating and sympathizing, have made some progress towards affiliation; but the main fact is as I have stated it. It is also true that pacific utterances have been heard, that courtesies have been interchanged with Northern military companies, and that Northern visitors (especially newspaper correspondents or distinguished men) have met with hospitality. But all these things have been merely formal, except in the case of the military, who have been actuated not by friendship or reconciliation, but by the chivalric sentiments of soldiers for gallant foes. These things have been done in the hope of obtaining relief from our bandit governments, or of gaining ascendency in the national councils.

Indeed, this leads me to observe that hatred for the North is often largely modified into hatred for the republican party; but the party attachment of the whites for Northern democrats is too much like that of hard-pressed soldiers for mutineers in the enemy's camp, to be a healthful sign of reconciliation. The lost cause, our trials during the war, our brilliant deeds in arms, our reverses, our grievances since the peace, form the staple of fireside and social conversation in every Southern family, and will do so for generations. Every child at its mother's knee is told of the brave old days; how its father used to own troops of slaves and counties of land; how he or some other honored relative fell under the banner of Morgan, of Lee, of Stonewall Jackson, or of Hampton; and into its mind is instilled hatred of their slayers and a resolution to avenge their death "some of these days." Shafts to the honor of the Confederate dead are thick in every grave-yard and cemetery, covered with tear-moving inscriptions; and once a year, on Memorial Day, the whole white population turns out,—suspending all business,—amidst the tolling of bells, to decorate the graves of their fallen heroes, and listen to eulogies and poems on them and the cause they died for. I do not reprobate the custom; it is only as natural as it is undeniable.

The Southern press teems with publications relating to the war—with the histories of Pollard and of Alexander H. Stephens (which are found in every white school as text-books), and rabid memoirs of Admiral Semmes, and lives without number of Lee and Jackson.[27] The historical societies, since the great speech of General Hill, have been busily collecting statistics justifying the prison management of the Confederate government, and proving that Confederate prisoners were worse used than Unionists.

It is true that democratic conventions and democratic leaders in the South have pledged themselves to abide by the issues of the war. But these utterances are worth no more than platforms and diplomatic professions in general. Beyond all things would Southerners rejoice to be free, to achieve their independence of the nation which has conquered them, of which they, *nolens volens*, must form a part.[28] But they have tested the strength of the North, and learned to dread it. Nothing could induce them to engage the North singlehanded again; and the more so, that they now have a possible intestine foe, the negro, to deter them. But contingencies may be easily imagined which would tempt them to rise; for instance, should they get the South solid, put the negro down at home, get him sufficiently intimidated or pacified to use as a Sepoy force, and a war should break out between the United States and some foreign power with which the South could side.[29]

There is another kind of contingency which seems likely to occur at no very distant period. The excitement in the South over the presidential contest is literally frightful. Should it be adverse to Mr. Tilden, the national House of Representatives and Mr. Tilden have it in their power to cause an explosion in the South so terrific that the outbreak of 1860-61 will be almost forgotten. The most dangerous hopes and emotions are agitating the bosom of every Southerner. At every street corner and fireside, on the steps of every store, you may hear men saying that the hour of the republicans is striking, they have got to submit, the North is split, and "We'll try them this time with Tilden and New York to help us."

Next to separation from the Union, the South would relish ruling the Union. Her representatives would be as intolerant as of old. Once solid, she will always remain solid. Mr. Nordhoff is in error with regard to the probability of a whig revival in the South.[30] As he says, there were, undoubtedly, thousands of men in the South before the war who were conservative and opposed to secession; but they were dragooned into conformity by the fire-eating element then, and can be dragooned again; and, besides, many of them have become alienated from the North in consequence of having participated in Southern reverses, and they could hope to do nothing in the face of the popular animosity engendered by the strife. The fire-eaters would rule and keep the white vote consolidated, and thus hope to govern the Union through divisions in the Northern vote; for they are confident that the North cannot be kept as solid as the South.

Three evils are to be chiefly dreaded under Southern ascendency at Washington. The first is a tremendous rush of office seekers and bonanza jobbers from the South. Thousands of Southerners, not reared to exertion, have been compelled to struggle hard for a living since the war, and would, of course, naturally abandon uncongenial or ill-paying avocations for the delights of office; and from the willingness to get all the spoils possible *there would be a great clamor all over the South for internal improvements.* The second is the much-talked-of danger of the payment of Southern claims, compensation for the slaves, assumption of the Confederate debt, etc.[31] The Southerners, I know, would undoubtedly be overjoyed could these things be accomplished; but they fear that any attempt to accomplish them might rouse the North so powerfully that they would be put down decisively, and kept down. They consider the attempt unsafe; but here, again, the question is one of expediency, not of principle. Attempts would probably be made to carry the same points indirectly. The third, and, in my opinion, the most formidable evil would be the danger of a warlike foreign policy. The spirit of the South—and especially of the leading element, the aristocracy—is at present dangerously martial. The Southerners, naturally spirited, fond of hunting and the turf, and devotees of the code, took astonishingly well to war; reared as gentlemen, relieved from labor by their slaves, and utterly unaccustomed to steady exertion, they have repined much against the hard fate which has forced them to work like other people for a living; and the vast majority of them, bursting with impatience under their restraint, would gladly hail the excitement and dangers of a campaign as a refreshing intermission, a picnic as it were, in the dreary monotony of the remorseless struggle for existence. The Southern papers were vehement for war with Spain about the Virginius matter, and have been bitter against the president on account of his non-aggressive policy towards Mexico.[32] "Tilden will stop these incursions on the border" has been a frequent editorial remark. In social intercourse, I have heard dozens of influential Southern gentlemen exclaim, "Wouldn't it be glorious if we could have two new Southern States—another Texas from the Mexican territory, and Cuba from Spain!" There is, furthermore, the hope that in the event of war the South could secede if she chose, or confirm her sway over the Union by threatening to join the enemy.

The hostility with which the whites regarded the enfranchisement of the negro has made itself felt in the sternest ostracism of Southerners who have turned republican, even if they were sincere and shunned office. In this State the negro legislature is called the menagerie, and is never referred to without a malediction. It is true that the whites have at times (noticeably in

1874) voted for negroes for office, and even high office; but it was done only to escape confiscation. Large numbers of irreconcilables refused outright to do it, and were secretly admired by those who yielded, and openly applauded by the ladies. When the bolters in 1874 spoke at one time of nominating a negro for governor, the only daily journal then in Charleston, the leading democratic paper of the State and the South, said that South Carolinians might contrive to put up with a colored lieutenant-governor, but could not stomach a colored executive; there was a line which might God forbid they should ever pass.

Colored politicians, who can be distinguished by their shiny, dressy appearance, have always been held in detestation; their appearance is the signal for wrathful silence, scowls, and derisive winks; if one of them, in the open air, passes a group of young white men, either silence falls on them till he is past, or they burst into laughter and jeer him as long as he remains in sight.

The intimidation and killing of negroes during election campaigns is a lamentable but significant sign. Negro citizenship rests solely on the very insecure support of United States bayonets; in this matter, again, the whites are guided by expediency alone. Whenever they dare, the whites in the Southern States will disfranchise the negro outright and by law; and in the mean while they will, in States they control, practically disfranchise him. For instance, the negro always evades paying taxes—even a poll-tax—as long as he can, and is notoriously given to roost-liftings, stealing cotton by night, killing hogs, etc., in the woods; accordingly, I am not surprised to see that in Georgia non-payment of taxes—even the poll-tax—is made to disfranchise a voter, that half the negroes are already disfranchised for non-payment, and that every man in Alabama convicted of larceny is disfranchised. White employers object to their hands taking time to vote, and one discharged for this reason cannot obtain reëmployment. Young bravoes turn out upon election day, and jeer at, bully, or force negroes coming to vote into fights. In some riotous districts of Georgia, which the democrats now carry by the significant majority of eighty thousand, not a negro vote is polled; the increase of the democratic majority in Alabama since the State fell into democratic hands is well known. In Georgia there are no colored state officers, not even constables or police, and a negro has not been summoned to serve on a jury there for years; there is only one colored man in the legislature. An educational qualification, which is loudly clamored for in some Southern States, would disfranchise ninety-five negroes out of a hundred; and though many poor whites would murmur at such a measure, the fire-eaters would quickly bring them round by a judicious use of the cane and the pistol. So I should not be surprised to see that plan adopted in the Southern States before long.

The whites, I believe, will never attempt to reënslave the negro, even should they get out of the Union, or the North refuse to interfere. The matter is often in people's minds, as may be judged by the recurrence of such remarks as "I wonder what will be the end of this thing?" "What must we do with the negro?" etc. But reënslavement presents great difficulties and dangers. The negroes would resist it to the death: kill women and children, use the torch freely, flee to the swamps, and thence sally out to fight and ravage, so dearly have they come to prize their liberty. And even should they be ultimately subjected, there would be daily and nightly outbreaks, keeping the whites in constant suspense. But it is unmistakable that the inexpediency, not the wrong of the measure, would constitute the obstacle. The whites clearly regard subordination in all things as the natural condition of the negro.

Should the North ever grant free play, or a separation occur, I should look for the whites to go as far as they dare in restricting colored liberty by black codes or detached laws, without actually re-establishing personal servitude. For instance, from the irritation felt in consequence of the stealing and selling of cotton at night, and their incursions into chicken, meat, and potato houses, and barns, we may expect negroes to be prohibited from stirring from home at night after some curfew hour, save under patrol or police regulations. From the animosity evinced towards their Union Leagues, political clubs, mass-meetings, etc., we may look for the prohibition of all colored assemblages; their churches would probably be put under police espionage, to prevent the discussion of political themes. From the great irritation felt at colored men who support their wives in idleness, or send their children (needed to work on the plantation) to school, we should anticipate astringent vagrant laws, and laws forbidding colored children to attend school during work hours, if at all. From the exasperating disposition of the negro to quit employers before his time is out, and to work unsteadily while employed, we may predict laws prescribing the manner in which they shall hire themselves (perhaps requiring strict contracts, holding them to labor for stated periods at stated wages), severely punishing idleness *and making the violations of contract by a negro a penal offense.* Bills of that purport have been introduced into the Georgia legislature, and voted down as premature. Finally, from the delight with which the killing of a negro leader is hailed who shows any signs of becoming "dangerous" through his intelligence or culture, it is easy to foresee that whites would be lightly punished (if juries would ever convict them) for crimes against blacks, while the criminal law would be severe on black offenders, and convictions easy.

The Union Leagues gave the negroes their first notions of parliamentary law and debating. They were encouraged to attend courts as spectators, were inducted into jury and militia service, and their prominent men were elevated to office. For several years—until 1872—in this State they unresistingly followed the guidance of their white friends. There was little debate at their meetings, and most measures were passed unanimously. On juries, in the legislature, etc., they were sheepish, quiet, awkward, and docile. But gradually they began to pick up hints and to see things for themselves. They became ambitious for office and distinction, acquired confidence, joined in debate, and criticized the measures proposed by their white leaders; and for a few years past they have been growing the most irrepressible democrats it is possible to conceive. They delight in attending, either to mingle in or to look on at, all sorts of assemblages,—church services and meetings, political clubs and conventions, mass-meetings, the courts,—as well as to serve on juries or in the militia. They are astonishingly quick at imitation, and are a mere second edition of the whites. At their gatherings all have something to say, and all are up at once. They have a free flow of language, and their older men exhibit a practical, get-at-the-facts disposition (narrow-minded of necessity, yet intense from that very circumstance) which is a near approach to that sterling English quality, hard common sense. They are to the last degree good-humored unless persistently opposed, when they become excited, demonstrative, and violent, in both demeanor and language. While they are speaking, their orators are subjected to all kinds of interruptions,—questions, impertinences, points of order, etc. Consequently much disorder prevails at their meetings. In the legislature knives and pistols have been drawn, and members have been expelled for disorderly conduct.

The negroes undoubtedly have a genius for intriguing. They understand all the arts of the lobby. They are quick with points of order—tack on riders, hurry jobs through under the previous question, etc. They understand well how to make corporations pay for bills, and candidates for nominations. Rings are well known in their politics. They have gerrymandered the congressional districts so as to deprive the whites of two representatives they might fairly elect. To insure the elections, they have refused to pass laws providing for registration, as the constitution directs; and under this safeguard (every voter being allowed to vote at any precinct whatever in his county, if he swears that he is voting for the first time) they have rivaled in repeating any feats of Tammany or Philadelphia roughs. Charleston County has been chiefly the theatre of these deeds. Negroes in swarms go voting from poll to poll in the country, and then enter the city and vote at several precincts there. Negroes do this all over the State on a smaller scale, and they frequently cross from county to county to vote; while the voting, or attempts to vote, of boys under twenty-one is notorious. Until 1874 their managers also proved themselves adepts in packing ballot-boxes, or in manipulating returns; such frauds being easily detected by keeping lists of how many negroes and how many whites voted, the voting having generally been on the color line. The meetings of bolting republicans are frequently packed by regulars, their orators hissed, resolutions voted down, and their opposite carried.

The negroes moreover are as intolerant of opposition as the whites. They expel from the church, ostracize, and, if they can, mob and kill all of their own, though not of the white race, who would turn democrats; and they have done so ever since the war. The women are worse than the men, refusing to talk to or marry a renegade, and aiding in mobbing him. They treat bolting republicans in the same way. But in some counties the bolters at times, happening to outnumber the regulars, have proceeded to reverse the game, and intimidate the regulars into conformity. Charleston County for many years has had two republican factions waging relentless mob war on each other, the division originating in the rivalry of two noted white leaders.[33] When a negro does turn democrat, he surpasses the most rabid fire-eaters in violence, and on every occasion delights to banter, insult, or bully republican negroes, if white men are near to protect him.

On national questions the negroes, as is well known, implicitly follow the dictation of Northern republicans; but in home matters they are more independent. For three or four years they have displayed great dissatisfaction with their white leaders. "Our votes keep the party in power," they say, "and we ought to have the offices." In consequence, many white leaders have been discarded, and those who yet retain prominence have had to use money and official patronage freely to retain their influence. Out of about one hundred and twenty-five republicans in the two legislative houses last session, about one hundred and ten were colored. I speak from memory, but am substantially correct.[34]

The negroes have been accused of being easily led by demagogues; but they really rule the demagogues, not the demagogues them. Let the politicians do anything which is distasteful, and opponents spring up in every quarter. They are extremely jealous of any one's assuming to dictate to them. They are impatient of trespasses and domiciliary visits to a degree only exceeded by the English races, and often resist search-warrants. They also resist arrests, and have to be vigorously clubbed. One thing, though, must be mentioned. Their fear of being reënslaved offers a means by which dexterous politicians can often impose on them. If you can prove to their satisfaction that any measure will tend to give the whites any advantage over them, it is instantly quashed and its opposite forthwith carried, *nem con.*[35] The intense love the negro has acquired for liberty was conspicuously manifested in the recent canvass, when it became apparent that the whites were determined to carry the election on the Mississippi Plan, and, as the negroes thought, rob them of liberty. As to the negro's capacity for government, I must say frankly that he is no more fit for it than a crowd of Irish roughs picked up promiscuously in the streets of a Northern city.

*A South Carolinian.*

# South Carolina Morals

*The Atlantic Monthly* 39, No. 234 (April 1877)

WHILE AT THE CENTENNIAL, last summer, I fell into conversation with an old lady (a Northerner) on the street cars. I am, I console myself, eminently peaceable and Christian-like in appearance. "Where are you from?" said she. "From South Carolina," I replied. She started, "What?" she exclaimed; "why, you look just like other people!"

In morals the Southern whites respect and profess to obey the same great fundamental laws as the Northerners and other whites. There are plenty of men among us who can hear the decalogue and feel no self-reproach, and there are also many earnest Christians of blameless, self-sacrificing lives; but it is not to be denied that there are certain peculiarities of the Southern people, arising from their situation and circumstances, past and present,—though chiefly past,—which seriously affect their moral conduct. In all ordinary cases Southerners act morally quite like other people; but whenever the line of conduct to which they are urged by one of their peculiarities comes under the prohibition of a moral law, they are very apt to disregard that law altogether and go ahead, or put such a forced construction on it as will justify their actions. The peculiarities referred to are three in number: (1.) Dissipation and the doctrines of the code of honor largely prevail among Southerners. (2.) Southerners have slender regard for the rights of the negro. (3.) They are unusually intolerant of opposition or of difference of opinion, especially in regard to political matters.

(1.) The planters of the South used to exhibit in the strongest form the virtues and the vices of all aristocracies. The typical Southerner possessed a liberal and chivalric cast of character which was founded mainly on family distinction, social culture, exemption from toil, and command over the lives and fortunes of his underlings. He would, for example, make large presents to waiters at hotels, or to the domestics at private houses, where he stopped. He was exceedingly fond of standing treat; he was frank and warm-hearted, strong in his attachments and dislikes, and would stick closer than a brother to a friend in trouble. By his generosity in lending money and going security he was often involved in embarrassment. He was noted for devotion to women, and for personal bravery even to rashness. He was fond of late suppers and choice wines, and delighted in hunting and in the sports of the turf and the pit. Truth was held in the highest estimation, and the least appearance of equivocation would condemn a man to utter disrepute; to give the lie was the worst of insults. He was often engaged in affairs of honor, for to take an insult was an everlasting disgrace; and being quick to resent insults or their appearance, he was equally hasty in offering them when excited or aggrieved; and although he might repent of having said unjust things and apologize a moment after to an honorable opponent, yet nothing could induce him to back out of a contest when he believed himself wronged. Careless of his own money, he was inclined to be careless in all pecuniary affairs, often running heavily into debt and showing habitual negligence in settling small accounts.

These characteristics, originating with the planters, were imitated by all orders. A reputation for gallantry and generosity became highly esteemed in the South. In consequence, many individuals in their efforts to attain it degenerated into bravoes and spendthrifts; the character of the fire-eater became almost as much admired as that of the gentleman. The passing of high words and blows, canings, cowhidings, and so on, all terminated by the drawing of knives or pistols, together with hostile correspondences and duels, became every-day occurrences in the South, and especially in South Carolina and perhaps Mississippi.

Now in a community where men are quick to wipe out insults with blood, the first effect is naturally to make individuals highly respectful to one another in manner and speech. This effect was very apparent in the conduct of most Southerners on ordinary occasions. But it is soon perceived that this politeness springs from fear, and then many persons of sensitive or hectoring dispositions will make their conduct habitually aggressive to prove they are not cowards, or to gain admiration. Every Southerner knew that if he preserved his temper and forgave insult on trying occasions, people would say he did it because he feared the pistol of his adversary; hence it became fashionable for every gentleman to act aggressively now and then, and perhaps to fight a duel, and having "vindicated his courage" to keep quiet on the strength of it. Many men, however, were so sensitive about the public condemning them should they make it a rule to be respectful towards opponents (say, in the legislature, at the bar, on the stump, or in the sanctum), that they became professional bullies, *always* acting and speaking insultingly to prove they were not afraid to fight. It was an almost indispensable qualification, certainly a desirable accomplishment, in a legislator, congressman, or editor, to have fought a duel. Consequently the fire-eating element came to preponderate among the statesmen who ruled us or whom we sent from home. The Southern *gentleman* was celebrated for his affable manners to all, rich and poor, black and white, while the fire-eater was sullen and dogged in his salutations; except when "showing off," he would hardly speak to negroes or whites lower in station than himself at all, and he was continually imagining insults and picking quarrels. A disregard for inflicting pain and shedding blood became lamentably common. All, even boys but just in their teens, were in the habit of wearing a pistol, as the slightest provocation would ordinarily reveal. It became well-nigh impossible to get a jury to convict any one (especially an aristocrat) of the most evident murder, provided he had exhibited daring in committing it, or had given his victim a chance to defend himself.

It also became a sign of gentility to be wasteful of money, to wager on every occasion and about everything, to stake high amounts, to run into debt, etc.; and it was thought to the last degree degrading for a man to be niggardly in lending money or indorsing for others. But the practical exhibition of such traits has, since the war, been much limited by the want of funds and the necessity of working for a living. Southerners still make largesses to servants, stand treat, game, and run into debt; but they can ill afford to be lavish with their money. Fees and bets are small in amount, and the aristocrat who of old would not wait to receive change, or who would pocket it without looking at it, will now count it over when handed him. Treats are as often invited as proffered, and cheaper refreshments are selected than formerly. Nine men out of ten carry pistols, and personal difficulties, castigations, stabbings, and shootings are yet entirely too common. But there have been only eight or ten duels in South Carolina since the war,—hardly as many as used to occur every year. Men will rarely fight duels when death may mean starvation to their families; and I ought to add that from the same cause pistols are not drawn so quickly as of old, and the tendency is to brandish rather than to shoot, so little can our hot bloods now afford the expenses of a legal trial; though it is still true that juries, both white and black—where the slayer and the slain are the same race—exhibit a strong disposition to let men off who have shown courage in committing crime.

The financial downfall of the aristocracy caused much loss among their creditors; and so the plebeian merchants and others, who used to rival each other in seeking the patronage of influential families, are now cautious to excess in dealing with them. The struggle for existence is undoubtedly working its effects on Southern character. Our business men, who used to ape the free and easy manners of the aristocrats, are now more practical. There is more caviling in making bargains. And even in the quiet streets of Charleston, once so noted for the easy-going appearance of their walkers, there are plainly discernible changes denoting the oncoming of "that hurried and high-pressure existence," which Mr. Greg so earnestly deplores.[1]

Adversity has produced, too, all its customary demoralization. Thousands upon thousands of Southerners were forced into *bona fide* bankruptcy after the war. But thousands who were better off made the prevalence of insolvency a cloak; and failures in business are well known to the lawyers to be yet too common. Women have been allowed to hold property independently of their husbands since 1868. Under the mask of this right, debtors are every day making over their property to their wives in order to cheat creditors. But worse than this, in every Southern State a few hundred or thousand individuals, who used to be as intolerant as their comrades, have at times since the war turned over to the republicans for the sake of office or plunder. These men have been dubbed "scalawags" and few are genuinely converted. Hundreds of whites, too, who were ardent in their support of the Confederacy have put in their claims as loyal citizens for losses sustained during the war. Many others knowing the legislature to be bribable, have used money to buy the passage of dishonest bonanza bills, by which they have made large amounts. Men, too, of high repute have lent their names to give respectability to rotten corporations, lotteries, and other enterprises designed to gull the people. And worst of all, the press has, in this State, been deplorably venal. Our corrupt rulers, fearing the papers might stir up the people to resistance—induce them, for instance, to refuse to pay taxes—did not scruple to invest hundreds of thousands of dollars in silly official advertising. Twenty democratic journals were once thus subsidized, and of course silenced.

Many Southerners were driven to drink deeply by their misfortunes, and drunkenness (with all the family misery it entails) is deplorably prevalent to this day. The taste for liquor is partly the effect of the warm climate, which requires stimulants.

(2.) It is a very common saying that the whites and negroes are at the bottom not unfriendly toward each other; that every white man loves his old "mauma," or faithful old family driver or servingman, while the negro is attached to his old "marsa" or "missis," who reared him, and with whom, perhaps, he has always stayed. This seems plausible. But there is a fallacy lurking under it. The whites are each of them fond of particular individuals among the blacks, but despise the race as a whole. And the same can be said of the blacks.

The whites are undoubtedly sentimentally attached to old family servants and certain acquaintances among the blacks. But towards other negroes their conduct is sullen and reckless; and for the rights of the race at large they have no consideration whatever, save what springs from compulsion. The old relations have not been forgotten. Every one thinks, and every child is trained up in the belief, that the negro is meant for the use of white people, was brought here and should stay here for no other purpose; and he is a half-way sort of animal, an excellent rice or cotton worker, an incomparable driver, waiter, or bootblack, but utterly incapable of government or culture; that he should be ruled in all things political, social, and industrial by the white man, should be kept in his place, and decisively suppressed if he tries to put on airs. I have seen whites who, actuated by religion or cowardice, were more passive under insult from other whites than Southerners are wont to be. But let a colored person insult them, and their nature seemed wholly altered. To swallow an insult from a negro would be perpetual infamy. Accordingly, the whites do not think it wrong to shoot, stab, or knock down negroes on slight provocation. It is actually thought a great point, among certain classes, to be able to boast that one has killed or beaten a negro. It is quite impossible to convict a white of a crime against a colored man if there be a white man on the jury.

Difficulties between whites and blacks in this State had been, until the recent presidential campaign, decreasing in frequency. The negroes had learned to invoke the law. And so freely had they indicted the whites for assaults and batteries (first before the military tribunals, and then in the state courts), that a very wholesome cautiousness had been engendered in the latter. The military were, of course, disposed to put down fire-eating; and the state justices or circuit courts (with their colored magistrates and juries) are very unsafe places for a white man. This cautiousness, too, has been increased by the prevalence of arson. If a white incurs the enmity of a negro, he is a very bad business man if he does not keep his buildings insured. The negroes, though, are often abused and then paid not to prosecute the case. They will readily withdraw their affidavits for a small consideration.

It seems a rather strange fact that although the negroes are much stronger physically than the whites, the latter often get the better of them in fights where no weapons are used; while if weapons are used they stand no chance whatever. But on thinking, one sees it is not strange after all. The negroes yet retain their inbred dread of their old masters, and their old inbred dread of *striking whites,*—which used to be, of course, a heinous crime, and brought down a terrible punishment; while the whites, yet, as I have said, retain much of their native contempt for and readiness to dash on the blacks. The demeanor of the races in conflict, in fact, often makes me think there is a germ of truth in Herodotus's pretty tale of the suppression of the slave rebellion by the Scythians.[2] It is a well-known fact that the younger generation of negroes, who have grown up since the war, are much more bold in defying white people than those who were slaves.

Reverdy Johnson was startled and indignant at the atrocities of the Ku-Klux.[3] But a moment's reflection would have convinced him that their deeds were not so unnatural as, at first sight, he evidently regarded them. The Ku-Klux Klan with its night visits and whippings and murders was the legitimate offspring of the patrol. Every Southern gentleman used to serve on the night patrol, the chief duty of which was to whip severely any negro found away from home without a pass from his master.

There used to prevail in the South an inquisitorial, relentless determination to suppress the truth about the maltreatment of the slaves. Atrocities were frequently perpetrated, yet it was persistently asserted that the negroes were uniformly well treated, were contented and happy, and that all reports to the contrary were malicious lies invented by interested politicians or crazy fanatics. While there are few Southerners who could not have written an abler vindication of Uncle Tom's Cabin than its authoress, on every hand she was denounced as a busybody, a mischief-maker, a fanatic, a lunatic, a liar of the first magnitude; and yet I have heard Southerners, who in formal argument would deny the possibility of any and every event in her matchless *exposé*, in moments of jovial conversation relate with great gusto anecdotes of how in the good old times they used to hunt down runaway negroes with hounds and guns, brand them, beat them till senseless, and while patrolling at night flog negroes who had passes, "just to hear them beg and hollo." "But all that's gone now," they remark with a sigh, on concluding.

This same determination to keep back the truth is rampant to-day. The most horrible tales of negro murders which have ever appeared in radical sheets at the North would pale before the relation of incidents known to every white man in the South. The intimidation of the negroes is a stern and awful fact. Yet what do Southerners say about it? It is the bloody shirt, the lying inventions of unscrupulous politicians, the last gasp of carpet-baggery and radical deviltry. So bitterly do Southerners hate to have the truth come out that it is at the risk of his life that any man dares to speak it. When a political crime is committed, they palliate it, smooth over everything, charge the blame on the murdered victims, and indulge in loud generalities about their good feeling towards the negro, their desire for peace, their willingness to accept the situation. An ex-Confederate, a leader of the whites in this State, exclaimed when the news of the Hamburg Massacre arrived, "Hello, boys, glorious news! They've come down on 'em at Hamburg,—seven niggers killed! Hurrah for Butler!" A conservative white standing by suggested to him that it was a pity the men had been shot after surrendering. "Oh, damn your prisoners,—they were nothing but niggers." A few months afterwards this same gentleman tried to explain away the Hamburg affair to a garrison officer: "You see, we all regret such occurrences, but the negroes provoked the difficulty and it was unavoidable. The killing of the prisoners we all deplored, but the negroes had exasperated the men so they could not be restrained."

(3.) All aristocracies are intolerant. The planters of the South had their intolerance in political matters increased by the fear that opposition to their favorite opinions might rob them of their slave property, or cause the negroes to rise. The treatment of Garrison in Maryland is well known; after his removal to Boston the legislature of Georgia offered a reward for his apprehension, and he would surely have been lynched had it caused his extradition South.[4] The Kansas troubles, the beating of Sumner, and the terrible feeling stirred up by Brown's raid on Virginia need but a reference. Smart negroes were made away with like Helots, and the teaching negroes to read and especially to write was forbidden by law.[5] Native whites non-conforming in opinion—anti-slavery or Union men—had no security but in keeping quiet. If they made themselves conspicuous, they were certain to be so grossly insulted by some fire-eater that unless they appealed to the duello their influence was forever destroyed. The most striking instance I recollect was that of ex-Governor Perry, an aristocrat, but a Union man in his sentiments. He was at one time before the war editor of a paper which began to work mischief to the state-rights cause. A fire-eater who had a pistol case for hire was imported from a distance to edit a rival paper. He began a series of brutal but "spicy" personal attacks on Mr. Perry and his journal. Mr. Perry continued silent for a time, but at last, to avoid public scorn, he was compelled to resort to the duello. As it happened he killed his man and survived to be appointed provisional governor of the State by President Johnson. He evaded challenges afterwards on the ground that he "had vindicated his courage."[6] No anti-Calhounist could speak out in the legislature or on the forum but some fire-eater would take him up so aggressively that a duel was the only escape from disgrace.

But not in politics alone was intolerance evinced. The aristocrats were also intensely clannish, and would endure no rivalry from plebeians. For instance, at the local colleges the secret fraternities fell into the hands of aristocratic students who excluded all others. Their organizations were then used to control elections in the literary and debating societies, to which all the students belonged, and in the classes. The high offices were given to aristocrats, and aristocrats were appointed to deliver the valedictories and salutatories. If a plebeian student of talent made himself prominent, cold water was thrown on all he did, and it was not unlikely, if he gave promise of winning the first honors or other high prizes, that such a cry would be raised against him as to cause his withdrawal from the race, if not from college. Duels were more common at Southern than at German colleges and universities; and a very ordinary way of putting down plebeians was by forcing them into affairs of honor through bitter personalities in debate or scurrilous remarks made to reach their ears. In practical life the same thing appeared. The aristocrats often *ex gratia* would elect a prominent or smart plebeian to office, if he were content to dance attendance.[7] But if he essayed independence, he was promptly sent to Coventry or insulted till forced to fight or subside. The aristocrats relentlessly crushed any "unworthy" member of their own circle who tried to violate their customs and traditions. Plebeians chancing to give offense to the planters had their negroes whipped and mutilated without cause by aristocratic patrolmen,—to incapacitate them for work, damage their market value, or out of pure spite and bravado,—or had a crowd of arrogant hunters tear down their fences at night and chase a fox through their fields, to the immense damage of the crops. This oppression was naturally imitated, as far as practicable, by the lower classes, each of which kept up a caste system among its own members, and rode over the classes below.

Since the war, authority has repressed political tyranny to a considerable extent. But it is yet rife, and a relaxation of authority is instantly followed by its aggressions. The ostracism of white republicans, native or Northern, is rigid, and it breaks out into deadly persecution when opportunity offers. The Ku-Klux beat and killed white republicans as vindictively as negroes; indeed more vindictively, as the remark was common, "Put away their leaders, and we can soon bring the negroes to terms." Especially were they violent against school-teachers and "propagandists" of Northern birth; and during the canvasses on the Mississippi plan, the intimidation of white republicans is equally severe with that of colored. The editor of the first republican newspaper founded in this State after the war was twice horsewhipped, so unaccustomed were the people to the liberty of the press.[8] I should here remark that a fighting editor is absolutely indispensable to a Southern paper. The slightest personality is apt to result in an attempt to chastise the editor; and yet the editors, knowing the public will attribute moderation to fear, are generally very acrimonious.

The desire of the aristocracy to keep down plebeians is as strong as ever, though poverty has much restricted its indulgence. Many impoverished aristocrats just after the war, in danger of being sold out by their creditors, excited such feeling on the subject that the creditors would compromise at great loss rather than subject themselves to peril by proceeding. Nevertheless, many old family homesteads were put under the hammer; but in not a few instances, by the free use of threats, bidders were frightened off, thus enabling the owners to bid in their own property at a nominal price. I am familiar with one case in which a wealthy plebeian merchant was brave enough to attend such an auction and participate in the bidding. The aristocrats present were furious, said the thing was an outrage, and told the owner to bid higher than he had intended or was able, as they would lend him the money; but the merchant had more than their united means, and secured the estate. A short time afterwards, while driving out with his sister, he was set upon by a kinsman of the aggrieved aristocrat, pulled out, and cruelly beaten. In September last a merchant foreclosed a lien he had on the crop of a planter's widow in _____ county. He did it because she was pursuing the usual aristocratic course of evading payment and putting him off. The indignity threw the lady into convulsions which caused her death. She was hardly buried before her three grown sons, all under twenty-five, were mounted and on their way to the merchant's. They found him in a lawyer's office in town, put everybody out but him, and closed the door. His screams and cries for mercy alarmed all the village. A crowd collected, and tried to interfere. But one of the young men came out on the steps with a cocked pistol in each hand, and kept them off till the victim was insensible, beaten to a jelly, gashed all over, and had one ear cut off. They then came out and rode off. The merchant lay at the point of death for weeks, is yet (two months since the fray) in bed, and is maimed for life. The affair was mentioned in no paper, and the young men have never been indicted.

But the aristocracy have been compelled to unbend considerably. Plebeians advance money on their crops, own mortgages on their lands, employ their sons as clerks, etc. Furthermore, plebeians own most Southern property now, since the gentlemanly aristocrats have taken ill to money making, to which the plebeians are used. So the commercial classes are beginning to acquire something like their normal position, with all the respect due to it, though the aristocrats choke it down hard.

The negroes also believe in and profess to practice the usual moral code. But in obedience to moral laws they are far less advanced than the whites; and there are, in their case, certain peculiarities produced by past or present circumstances which often lead them to disobey or pervert their theories of right. For instance, the negro used to know that he was wrongfully held in slavery, and did not scruple to feign sickness in order to avoid work, or to lay hands on any article of his master's which he could appropriate without being detected. These things continue, though their cause is removed. It is not considered wrong among negroes to steal from or in any manner cheat whites. They trespass for wood in forests, or take rails and planks off fences. Their nightly depredations are notorious. No work can be got from them unless they are superintended. Hired laborers take too many holidays, are sick half the time, and in every way shirk work. The stealing propensity is the bane of the negroes in politics. They know that their legislators and other officers steal the public deposits, but, knowing the whites pay the taxes, they applaud the theft, and every one is eager to be elected so that he may have a share in the spoils. Prominent negroes (I know myself of a congressman and a state senator who have done it) have frequently made incendiary speeches, saying the taxes should be raised till the whites are ruined and property depreciated in value, when lands sold for delinquent taxes can be bid in at low rates by colored men, who will soon have all the country to themselves. These men, on being accused of advocating confiscation, openly acknowledge it, and justify themselves by saying that the whites used to steal their wages, and now the negro's time has come.

Lying is at this day the negroes' worst failing. They are the most bare-faced perjurers ever seen in courts of justice; and especially are they experts in giving false testimony to save fellow blacks prosecuted by whites.

It is perhaps well that the carpet-baggers assumed their leadership, as their passions, which might otherwise have sought gratification in blood, were thereby diverted almost exclusively to plunder. The readiness of white men, indeed, to use the pistol has kept them respectful to some extent, though, as I have said, they fearfully avenge any grievances from whites by applying the torch to out-buildings, gin-houses, and often dwellings. But to white children they have been extremely insolent and threatening. White ladies have to be very prudent with their tongues, for colored domestics give back word for word, and even follow up words with blows, if reprimanded too cuttingly. It has also since emancipation been notoriously unsafe for white ladies to venture from home without an escort.

The possession of weapons greatly added to negro insolence. They have delighted from the outset to carry weapons demonstratively, to trespass on forbidden premises for game, etc. If a negro is overcome in a fight by a white man, those of his race present will dash in to aid him. The white spectators will then interfere to help their comrade, and a free fight is often the result. The beating of a white by a black produces white interference, followed promptly by colored interference. And in collisions between whites and blacks the friends of the respective parties think themselves bound to interfere, *not to stop the fight*, but to help out their comrade. If a white man shoots a colored man, an excited mob of blacks will try to lynch him. His friends rally to the rescue, and there is often a riot. The conditions are reversed if a white man is shot by a negro. The existence of so vindictive a spirit between the races convinces me that the presence of United States troops is often essential to peace and good order in the South.

The negroes outdo Squire Western in the use of filthy language, and the women are as foul-mouthed as the men, and as profane.[9] Chastity is the exception among them. Tens of thousands of negroes live together as man and wife without marrying. The married ones are every day quitting each other and taking up with illicit partners. I trust I shall be excused for referring to the above facts. Had I omitted to do so I should have left untouched one of the most momentous features in the sociology of the South.

The negro in ordinary relations with both his own and the white race is good-natured to jollity; but arouse his passions and he is terribly revengeful. They quarrel and fight savagely with each other. Murders are frequent, and they mutilate persons (white or black), whom they kill, in a shocking manner. The women in their rage are tigresses.

Most of the equity and civil business (though our chancery affairs are administered by the law judges) in our courts is supplied by the whites. But the bulk of the criminal business is supplied by the blacks. A white is rarely seen in a Southern court for any crime other than murder or assault and battery. Whenever larceny, burglary, arson, and similar crimes are committed in the South, no one is suspected of the crime save negroes. Out of three hundred and fifty-five prisoners now in our state penitentiary, three hundred and twenty-five are colored! The negro is fanatical in his religion, but deplorably loose in his morals; and though his animal passions are largely repressed by the idea of a God of vengeance, and the terrors of hell set before him every Sunday, yet these theoretical restraints need to be supplemented by swift and terrible legal penalties for every transgression,—that is, as long as the negro continues as he is. But I sincerely trust some means will be found to elevate him to a higher moral plane by education.

My account would be incomplete were I to omit mentioning two considerations which account for the vices of the negro. The first is this: so often were the slaves whipped and humiliated before each other, often for no cause, that punishment came to be looked on as no disgrace. This sentiment, I am sorry to perceive, has survived the fall of slavery. Imprisonment, even for degrading crimes, like stealing, is looked on as no disgrace, and the moment the convict leaves the jail or penitentiary he resumes the place in colored society that he left, finds himself for a week the object of general interest as he discourses on his adventures in the great "penny-tenshun" in the far-off city they have so often heard mentioned, begins life anew, and is treated as if nothing had happened. Discharged convicts have often been elected to the legislature! The second consideration is the prevalence of drunkenness. I fear drink is destined to prove as much the bane of the negro as of the Indian. All his earnings with which he might make home comfortable or increase his property are spent for it. It intensifies his quarrelsomeness, disposition to mob whites, bad treatment of his family, etc. Every Saturday afternoon the negroes swarm into the towns from the country, and as far as their means will permit indulge in potations of poisonous whisky. On these occasions street fights and riots are the invariable results. The negro women, unluckily, are almost as much given to drinking as the men.

But the negroes are not without example. Intemperance, owing perhaps to the climate, has always been as notoriously a failing of the Carolinas as of Kentucky itself; and the war has increased it as mentioned before. In drunken brawls the whites rival the negroes.

*A South Carolinian.*

# South Carolina Society.

*The Atlantic Monthly* 39, No. 236 (June 1877)

SOUTH CAROLINA was first successfully colonized in 1669, under the government of the lords proprietors. Afterwards colonists came over freely from England, France, and elsewhere. Those from England predominated, and were composed of two widely differing classes; first, Roundheads who wished to leave England—then passing through the corrupt era of the Restoration—and find a place where liberty of conscience was granted; and secondly, Cavaliers, impoverished by the Revolution, whom the king, for want of better means, had rewarded for their fidelity by grants of large tracts of land in the New World. Every religion was tolerated in South Carolina, but the Church of England was established as the state church. The sultry climate impaired the efficiency of white laborers. So, only a year or two after the first settlement, negro slaves were brought from the Barbadoes. They proved useful, and were at once imported so rapidly as soon to exceed the white population almost as two to one. Planting, with African labor, became the favorite occupation. Rice was naturalized and extensively cultivated.

The planters, who were chiefly the Cavalier immigrants, soon constituted a regular landed gentry. They resided on their estates, erected imposing mansions, kept fine dogs and horses, and hunted over their vast demesnes, on which game abounded, especially foxes and deer, in the true style of English noblemen and squires. The law of primogeniture was preserved for over a century. The fashions of England were imported for the ladies, and the young men were sent over the water to pass through the English universities. Tea, coffee, chocolate, and delicious wines were kept on the tables, and every Sunday the ladies turned out in coaches driven four in hand, with the gentlemen galloping along outside on horseback, to hear their loved Anglican service read in the tasteful rural churches.

Such was the origin of the famous Palmetto aristocracy. Of course the planters were not noble by law (though it is a fact that under Locke's constitution several *bona fide* nobles were created with the title of landgrave), but socially and industrially they were a nobility, and politically they wielded such influence as to make them practical nobles. The rice planters were the aristocracy till after the Revolution. But after the invention of the cotton-gin, in 1793, the culture of cotton received a tremendous impulse, and it was erelong as much the staple of South Carolina as rice. So the aristocracy soon included as many cotton as rice planters.

There was also a landed nobility in colonial Virginia; and with this and that of South Carolina originated the *antebellum* aristocracy of the whole South, excepting, perhaps, Louisiana. But the Palmetto aristocracy undoubtedly set the type,—even the Virginians had to conform. For the old Southern aristocracy was characterized not only by the possession of lands but also of slaves; and "of the original thirteen States," says Bancroft, "South Carolina alone was from its cradle essentially a planting State with slave labor. In Maryland, in Virginia, the custom of employing indented servants long prevailed; and the class of white laborers was always numerous, for nowhere in the United States is the climate more favorable to the Anglo-Saxon laborer than in Virginia. It was from the first observed that the climate of South Carolina was more congenial to the African than that 'of the more northern colonies;' and at once it became the great object of the emigrant 'to buy negro slaves, without which,' adds Wilson, 'a planter can never do any great matter.'"[1]

Without detailing the development and spread of the system over the whole South, I propose to take it up as it existed in its prime just before the war, and describe its main features, together with those of the rest of Southern society.

The whites of the South, then, were divided into several distinct classes. There were, in general, the aristocracy, the respectable people, the working people, and the poor whites or sand-hillers. The aristocracy was founded on blood and wealth. A historical ancestry was indispensable; but if a "true blood" aristocrat became poor, though he would be turned down lower in his class, he would not be looked on as "degraded" to the class I have styled the respectable people. Culture would also gain a man influence among the aristocracy, but the lack of it would merely cause him to sink on the scale of his own circle, at the very foot of which he would still be immeasurably higher than a member of the respectable element. Pedigree, then, was essential. But the aristocrats were also powerfully distinguished in what I may call an industrial point of view. Some of them, from choice or from impoverishment, became lawyers, doctors, ministers, bankers, factors, wholesale merchants, railroad presidents. But the main body were slave-holding planters,—not *farmers*. These planters generally owned thousands of acres of land and hundreds of slaves. The census of 1860 shows that the average area of plantations in South Carolina was sixteen hundred acres. Some gentlemen owned four thousand slaves, and few members of the aristocracy owned less than two hundred. The planters employed their time in the chase, in dissipation, in study, in visiting, in the duties of hospitality, or, as was usual, became public men. Their estates were managed by overseers, who directed the agricultural operations and managed the slaves through colored deputies called "drivers." The houses of the overseers were placed near the "negro quarters," villages consisting of from ten to fifty or a hundred cabins, of either one or two rooms, and generally grouped around or near one or more spacious barns and stables, with a cotton-gin or two run by mule power, and a great compass screw.

The respectable people were known from the classes below them by their wealth and culture, and often were distinguishable from the aristocrats only by their lack of ancestral distinction; that is, there were many large planters among them. But usually when agriculturalists their plantations were small and their slaves few in number, so that they were called farmers in contempt. The respectable people, however, were mainly the commercial classes of the community,—merchants, clerks, corporation men, etc. Members of the respectable class were sometimes received into the aristocracy, although until several generations had elapsed it would be half on sufferance; sometimes plebeian planters would climb up to such high social eminence in regions where there were no aristocrats that they would become aristocrats by prescription, while influential plebeian families after a few generations of wealth and leisure (especially if they produced any distinguished men) were slowly recognized by the aristocracy. Of course among the respectable people there were various subdivisions, produced by degrees of wealth, education, or distinction, and they were by no means so strongly discriminated from the class below them, the working people, as from the aristocracy. A working man often climbed into the respectable class,—far oftener than a respectable man into the aristocracy—because descent was not a qualification, while wealth and culture, which *were* the qualifications, were of course attainable by energy. But still there was a general distinction. The respectable people, relieved from manual drudgery by their slaves, and imitating the airs of the aristocrats, looked with more than usual contempt on working people. This working class included men who (as a rule) owned no slaves, and had to labor for a livelihood with their hands,—carpenters, mechanics, farmers who did their own work, etc.

The poor whites lived on the sand hills in pine forests, as a general thing, though many of them also dwelt in the flat-woods. They were squalid, lazy, and extremely ignorant, almost as much despised as the blacks. They formed the pauper population of the South.

The residences of the planters were easily discerned by their size,—rarely having less than ten apartments,—their spacious verandas, and the lawn or park in front with its long lines and stately avenues of venerable oaks. They were generally constructed of wood, and in their rear was a kitchen, a group of negro huts, and at some distance a barn and ample stables. I will refer later to some urban features in the lives of the rice planters.

"The Southerner of pure race," says M. Michael Chevalier, "is frank, hearty, open, cordial in his manners, noble in his sentiments, elevated in his notions; he is a worthy descendant of the English gentleman. Surrounded from infancy by his slaves, who relieve him from all personal exertion, he is rather indisposed to activity, and is even indolent. He is generous and profuse. . . . To him the practice of hospitality is at once a duty, a pleasure, and a happiness. Like the Eastern patriarchs or Homer's heroes, he spits an ox to regale the guest whom Providence sends him and an old friend recommends to his attention; and to moisten this solid repast, he offers madeira—of which he is as proud as of his horses—that has been twice to the East Indies and has been ripening full twenty years. He loves the institutions of his country, yet he shows with pride his family plate, the arms on which, half effaced by time, attest his descent from the first colonists and prove that his ancestors were of a good family in England. When his mind has been cultivated by study, and a tour in Europe has polished his manners and refined his imagination, there is no place in the world in which he would not appear to advantage, no destiny too high for him to reach; he is one of those whom a man is glad to have as a companion and desires as a friend. Ardent and warm-hearted, he is of the block from which great orators are made. He is better able to command men than to conquer nature and subdue the soil. When he has a certain degree of the spirit of method, and, I will not say [of] will (for he has enough of that), but of that active perseverance so common [among his brethren] at the North, he has all the qualities needful to form a great statesman."[2]

The question now comes up, Has the influence of the aristocracy been impaired by the war? It undoubtedly has. Their undisputed dominance before the war was owing to three causes: (1) their immense possessions; they owned at least one half if not more of the two great articles of Southern property, slaves and land; (2) their lineage; and (3) their superior culture, social and intellectual.

Now the first cause was enough of itself to insure their ascendency. They owned most of the property and paid most of the taxes; and as the property-holding class in the South were the voters (most Southern States used to restrict the suffrage to citizens owning a freehold of not less than fifty acres, and require members of the legislature to possess a freehold of five hundred acres and own ten negroes) there was never a necessity of asking the body of the people what to do. But the slave property of the aristocracy has utterly gone; and three fourths of their real estate have passed into the hands of plebeians or negroes, while the rest is depreciated in value. In fact, their distinction as slave-holders and as land gentry has ceased. They have been forced to work with brains and hands, and are industrially reduced to the level of the other whites, of whom, apparently, they now form a part. So it would be impossible to say that they have not lost power.

Yet at this day, as of old, Southern aristocrats are our public men and statesmen, and the fire-eating policy has again prevailed all over the South.

The explanation is simple. While the industrial power of the aristocracy has been taken away, their ancestral distinction and their intelligence and social superiority to the mass of the whites have remained intact. They compose the highest circle of Southern society, which is looked up to and copied by all below, with how much awe words cannot tell. Then Southerners have a national character, well defined of their own; and whatever individual possesses in their strongest form the traits constituting that character is sure to attract popular admiration and acquire influence. Now the aristocracy were largely instrumental in molding this national character of the South, and its members exhibit Southern traits in their intensest form. So they are reverenced by the people, and are the popular heroes and leaders. The names of aristocrats still appear as the honorary members or trustees of every association, as the managers of public balls and entertainments. If a lyceum, a college literary society, or a political club wish an address delivered, they select an aristocrat—often venerable and known to history—as orator, and their hall is crowded with eager listeners. If a new joint-stock company is started, its success is assured if some members of the aristocracy can be induced to accept nominal positions as directors. The insurance companies invariably select ex-Confederate generals for their state agents, and their lower agents, as well as those of the sewing-machine companies, are members of the aristocracy. Gentlemen of the old school abound among us, can be told from all others by their indescribable air of cultivation and distinction, and are worshiped by the people. The aristocracy regard themselves, and are acknowledged, as select and deserving special consideration. As far as poverty will permit them, they keep up their old customs and traditions. Whenever an aristocrat is compelled to mingle with the respectable and working classes, they treat him with a respect which is positively amazing; there is a tacit understanding on both sides that he is among them but not of them, which, such is human nature, actually causes them to "boot-lick" or dance attendance all the harder. It is impossible to describe the fearful excitement produced when an aristocrat is hurt or killed in one of our numerous political fracases. One of the chief reasons why the whites turned over to the straight-out policy during the last campaign was in consequence of the passionate appeals made them after the Hamburg massacre not to desert their old general, Butler, whether he had done right or wrong, and leave him to fight his battles alone with Governor Chamberlain, whose kitchen organ in Columbia was crying out for Butler's arrest.[3]

As a consequence, the old divisions of Southern society yet exist. The aristocracy is discriminated from the respectable people, the respectable people from the working class, though less strongly than of yore, and all from the sand-hillers.

Then again the commercial men of the South, the respectable people, perhaps have never had anything to do with politics. In old times they looked on politics with positive aversion as being something utterly unfitted for practical men, and so never mixed in political strife; for, as I explained in my paper on Morals, the old-time Southern politician had to be a "gentleman of honor" and a fiery orator. Now this is still the conception of a statesman in the South; that is, the popular ideal of a statesman is a man who is a polished gentleman, chivalric in his bearing, able to deliver eloquent addresses brimming with sharp denunciation and vehement exhortation, and who is ready to back up his words with the pistol. Our practical men, at least those old enough to lead, still dislike having anything to do with politics. They stay away from political conventions or take back seats. They decline nominations to office, while the aristocrats, still all fire and all born orators, are the very ones on whom the people look as the embodiment of statesmen; and not only do they come forward as candidates for positions as if nobody had a right to oppose,—as a matter of course,—but the people look on their doing so as eminently proper, and are aghast, scarcely less aghast than the aristocrats, if some presumptuous plebeian ventures to set himself up against them. In short, their political ascendency is yet looked on, and will long be looked on by the Southern whites as an unquestionable portion of the eternal fitness of things.

Then there remains their intellectual power. Fully one half—perhaps three fourths—of the educated men of the South (especially of the college-bred men) used to be aristocrats. Now when the aristocrats were forced to work after the war, to avoid starvation, they of course, as far as possible, selected brain work in preference to manual labor. They became lawyers, doctors, ministers, and teachers. Consequently over three fourths of the members of the learned professions in the South are aristocrats. Especially is the bar stocked with them, and lawyers generally have their way in politics. The colleges, too, ever since the war, have been eager to get aristocrats into their professorships. General Lee was made president of a famous college in Virginia. The Hon. Robert W. Barnwell, ex-United States senator from this State and the friend of Jefferson Davis, was made the head of the old South Carolina College when revived before reconstruction. I could mention dozens of other instances. But as I have said, the aristocrats turned teachers, too,—teachers of the schools. Hundreds of impoverished ladies of the aristocracy also became teachers in boarding-schools and grammar-schools for girls. I hardly exaggerate when I say that the training of Southern youth is now confided to the old aristocracy. They impress their manners and opinions on their pupils, and the consequence is that the rising generation of Southerners surpass their fathers in Southern bigotry and anti-Northism. I was actually about to omit mentioning that the press, with all its immense power, is also in the hands of the aristocracy; for of course the sanctum was as favorite a resort of impoverished aristocrats as school teaching, etc. I will merely instance the facts that the leading democratic daily of Charleston (the organ of Hampton, Butler, and the democratic central committee) is edited by Mr. R. Barnwell Rhett; and that the only democratic daily of Columbia is edited by Mr. C. P. Pelham, ex-professor in the college over which Preston and Barnwell have presided.[4]

The aristocracy, then, are yet the public men of the South. But whereas they used to drive the people before them with the lash and pistol, as it were, they are now merely guides, trusted and followed, indeed, and likely to be so for a considerable time, but whom the people can refuse to follow if they choose. Until the recent campaign, for instance, the people of this State insisted on the selection of very straight paths.

The great body of the aristocracy, as I have observed, were ruined by the war,—some steeped in poverty to the very lips at once. Not a few sank under the blow into insanity. Others were seized with apathy and despair. They lived on, as best they were able, selling their lands and personal property as necessity pressed them. Others went manfully to work. Plenty of high-bred and haughty women, widowed by the recent strife, hesitated not to enter the field and superintend their laborers. Most gentlemen discharged their overseers and managed their own estates. Young scions of the aristocracy hired out to their more fortunate neighbors as overseers, or scrupled not to become clerks, teachers, or depot, express, insurance, and sewing-machine agents. The ladies advertised for boarders, became teachers or governesses, or took in sewing. Those families who were not immediately prostrated contrived, as I have said, to drag on for a while. They persisted in retaining their carriages, drivers, and outriders, in giving stately family dinner-parties, in handing wine to visitors, in making formal visits. Gradually they descended. They became their own drivers, they opened their own gates. Their vehicles grew old and dingy. Their horses, at first kept solely for riding or driving, were worn out at the plow or sold; mules replaced them in the carriage. Their dinners were given at intervals few and far between. Their main solicitude became to avoid starvation. Many were compelled to do their own cooking.[5] Most of them waited on themselves. The merchants, after crediting them until ruinous amounts were lost, demanded cash. Many were sold out for private debts. Their efforts to keep up appearances have been often truly pitiable.

Since the war the people of South Carolina have had many old home associations broken up. Hundreds of houses were burned during the war; almost as many have since been fired by incendiaries. Bankruptcy was the universal order after the cessation of hostilities. Many have been sold out for taxes. Three fourths of the whites have had to change either their homes or their locality. This has caused much mental suffering. The negroes also have been incessantly moving. The great majority left their old owners. They are very troublesome servants to keep, so that they rarely remain anchored long in any one vicinage. Indeed, this leads me to say that one of the chief grievances of white ladies since the war has been the way in which house servants who leave them and hire to others gossip about them or slander them to their new employers. In old times, as every family had certain favorite old house servants who were never sold and always stayed with their owners, this annoying gossip was an unknown thing.[6]

The negroes generally took the family names of their owners on being set free; though a third or more of them, whose owners had been cruel, adopted the name of some former white master noted for kindness, or picked up names anywhere. They often bear distinguished names, and in police items one reads of Arthur Middleton being put in the guard-house for drunkenness, or Drayton Bull, Grimké Legaré, or Preston Laurens committed for petit larceny.

The carpet-baggers have been severely ostracized, socially, by the whites. The scalawags also, as the native white republicans are styled, have incurred the same treatment. The whites have insulted them and had nothing whatever to do with them, unless in the way of business or when there was an axe to grind. The same remarks will apply to the treatment of Northerners up to a year or so ago. But since then these last have met with far more attention, owing to political reasons, though the most superficial observer can detect that cordiality is by no means re-established. By Northerners I mean those who are not carpet-baggers; visitors, immigrants, or travelers.

The negroes generally still address the whites as Massa, Master, Boss, and Miss or Missis (for Mrs.), although, of course, all who are in politics or have money, together with not a few of the more insolent of the common mass, have dropped these titles for Mr. and Mrs. The main body of the colored people are inclined to be very respectful to the whites they know or are hired to. Occasionally a pert maid or man servant will address their employers as Mr. and Mrs. instead of Master and Miss, but the whites are very jealous of such innovations; I have known several nurses discharged because they refused to prefix Master to the names of the children. The whites call the negroes by their Christian names, except the elderly ones, who are called uncle or daddy, aunty or mauma. The negroes have commenced pretty generally to Mr., Mrs., and Miss each other. They are excessively fond of titles. Brother and Sister are also very ordinary appellations among them, and were made fashionable, I believe, by the Union League. It is esteemed disreputable among the whites to Mr. a negro, though of course it is frequently done when a white man has a bill to lobby through the legislature or other favor to request. The same remark will apply to touching the hat. As there are very few negroes (and these chiefly office holders) who are entitled to such rights by possessing such means and power as to raise them to the class of gentlemen, the difficulty rarely arises. The whites have many contrivances to avoid the use of such salutations. They will call a negro "Senator Smith," or "Sheriff Smith," or "Colonel Smith" to escape addressing him as "Mr. Smith." The papers have habitually avoided Mistering negroes, but do it occasionally for obvious political effect.

Whites will ride on the same seats in cars with blacks if the latter are traveling in the capacity of servants, nurses, etc. But they would die before doing the same if the latter were traveling as equals. The negroes, however, are permitted to, and frequently do ride in first class railway and in street railway cars. This liberty at first encountered much opposition from the railroad conductors and white passengers, and led to several fights, expulsions, and lawsuits. But it is now so common as hardly to provoke remark, although if a negro enters a car in which all the other travelers are white the latter, if they do nothing else, yet plainly evince aversion, and, if practicable, a wide space is left around such intruders. It is not often, though, that any of the blacks besides the politicians enter first-class conveyances on account of poverty; second-class tickets are purchased.

It is not thought wrong for a white baby to be suckled by its colored nurse. White children are always brought up with negro children as playmates. When the whites finish a meal, the colored servants remove the things to the kitchen and there eat from the same crockery the whites have just used. Yet, though all these familiarities—the most intimate imaginable—are not considered out of the way, the formal recognition of social equality is a thing as impossible as the production of the machine of perpetual motion; it is utterly, unutterably abhorrent to the Southern mind.

I do not believe that there are in the State a half dozen married couples with the wife white and the husband black or colored; but there are three or four instances in every county of colored women or negresses married to white men. So strong is the sentiment among the whites against such unions that few are, like Geoffrey Hunter, bold enough to wed with a Toinette.[7] It condemns them to bitter hatred and irrevocable social ostracism among their own race. They generally have no resource but to associate with the colored people and become negroes in all but color.

The negroes are freely admitted to the theatres in Columbia, and to other exhibitions, lectures, etc.; but a wide berth is given them by the white audience if the hall be not crowded. In Charleston and the country towns they have not thus far attended or secured entrance to such places. But to shows under canvas, such as circuses, magic-lantern exhibitions, and so on, they are invariably allowed admission. In Columbia, they are also served at the bars, soda-water fountains, and ice-cream soloons, but not generally elsewhere. From the hotels they are invariably excluded. In Columbia, Charleston, and the larger towns, they have their own boarding-houses; especially in the first place, where there are many officials, legislators, etc.

A white church in an up-country town wished to dispose of its lecture room in which the Sunday-school had been held. The county educational officials (some of whom were colored) bought it for a state school-house. It remained unused, however, for several months. About six weeks after its sale the white ladies in town proposed to give a concert. The lecture room was the only suitable hall in the village. Accordingly, the gentleman who was acting as their agent proposed to hire it for the occasion, after making a long explanation to them about its not having been used as yet by the radicals. But on hearing of this, one of the most prominent of the ladies instantly declined to have anything further to do with an entertainment which was to be given in a building owned by negroes. The concert was abandoned.

A widow in Marlborough, in destitute circumstances, desiring to send her son to Harvard, wrote to the president, and through his kindness, obtained favorable terms for tuition, etc. She was very grateful and in high spirits. At the last moment, however, a misgiving struck her. She dispatched another epistle, telling the president that she was *so* much obliged to him, and so forth, but that she had heard that negroes were in Harvard as students; and concluded by inquiring if it were true. The president sent a cold but courteous reply in the affirmative. The young man has never entered Harvard.

A very light mulatto, through a misapprehension, secured a night's lodging at a hotel in Chesterfield. The white guests forthwith departed. But on proper explanations being made by the proprietor, his patronage slowly revived.

The negroes (and by this term I mean both blacks and mulattoes) have among themselves social rank and aristocracy outrageously severe and strictly discriminated. This was the case even before the war, as Mrs. Stowe has noticed in her famous novel. These distinctions are local, so that no generalization could be made of the various classes. But the gradations are founded principally on official station, position in the church, possession of money or real estate, former ownership, and city birth. Those who have been trained up "genteelly" in white families of the highest respectability, as waiting men, maids, drivers, and so on, of course pride themselves not a little on their polished deportment; and those who are able to work on their own account (for instance, to rent land and to farm, to keep a smithy or to be carpenters) hold themselves considerably above such as have to hire out as laborers.

The whites are, like all other Americans, fond of military titles. The negroes, with their customary propensity to imitation, have become eager to procure commissions in the national guard, and to call each other captain and colonel and major.

In his family the colored man is tyrannical to the last degree. His wife generally cooks for him, and both, together with the children, hire out during the day. In order to prepare dinner no work is done from twelve o'clock to two. The negroes of the wealthier sort naturally imitate all the social customs of the whites, paying homage to the ladies, preventing the females from working, sending the children to school, living in fine houses, employing servants, supporting a good table, and keeping carriages and horses. The lower classes of negroes also copy, as far as they can, the habits of the whites. All are desirous of sending their children to the public schools, and contrive at intervals to do so, but the lack of means prevents a regular attendance,—the children must work. The whites have a violent prejudice, nay, hatred, against the laudable efforts at civilization, and take every opportunity to insult such negroes as make them. "Your wife and children had better be at work in the field," is a remark frequently heard. Of course, however, there is excuse for this feeling of the whites. The airs which the negroes assume often interfere with their efficiency as laborers, and give them a demeanor insolent and presumptuous; and to such novelties the whites are not yet accustomed.

The negro rarely possesses any home attachments. He is continually on the wing, as I have before remarked; and as he can with facility ingratiate himself among strangers of his own color, he would not be disconcerted were he as quickly transported from one State to another as Aladdin's wife or as Noured-din in the Thousand and One Nights.

The Southern gentleman yet displays much of his old chivalry of sentiment and behavior. Women are worshiped in the South by lovers and sons and gentleman-acquaintances, and they will prove in the end the chief obstacles to reconciliation with the North, as they are very conservative.

Every young man is afraid, if he associates with a Yankee or a republican, that his sweetheart will cut him, or his mother and sisters look grieved. The Southern lady, as a Northern authoress has recently observed, is usually far more helpless and fragile than her Northern sister. She is never allowed to do a thing if a gentleman is with her. Socially and politically, the state of women in the South is much less advanced than in the North. Nor is there much prospect of an amelioration. The idea of females voting or speaking in public is extremely distasteful to Southern whites, and even more so to the women than to the men. Southerners traveling in the North, and seeing ladies participate in public meetings, come back disgusted. A female lecturer from the North spoke in Charleston winter before last, but only a few rowdies went to hear her. The negro females are very roughly handled by the males, and colored children are treated by both their fathers and mothers in a way that would make Pestalozzi, Froebel, and Herbert Spencer shudder.[8]

The negroes used to be kept, as I have said, in cabins clustered together near the residence of their owner or his overseer. Since their liberation they have shown quite a tendency to desert these relics of their former subjection. Many of the "negro quarters," indeed, on isolated and *very* rural plantations are yet inhabited, but a large number all over the country are tenantless and going to ruin. Still more have been pulled down. A negro will buy a small lot of ground and erect on it a hut, the materials of which he has acquired by purchasing a cabin in a desolate "quarter" and pulling it down. They generally contrive to buy all their lots in one vicinity, and that just outside the borders of a town or village; so that every Southern town—at least this is the case in South Carolina—is divided into two sections: the main town, populated principally by whites, and containing the finest structures; and the "free town" (which the whites often dub "Liberia"), consisting chiefly of wretched log-cabins with wooden shutters, mud chimneys, and but one room. Of course most white families of affluence have in their yards inferior houses for the colored servants. Many maids even sleep in their employers' houses, although in such cases they are never assigned to a separate apartment (an attic, etc.) with beds, but pass the night on a pallet spread on the floor of the young mistress's chamber.

The food of the negroes is coarse and barbarously prepared, where they live apart from the whites. Their dwellings, as I have observed, have usually but one room, in which they sleep, cook, eat, sit, and receive company. Their culinary utensils, in most cases, consist simply of a large iron pot, an oven, and a few tin pans, all of which, most likely, have been previously well worn and thrown aside in the kitchens of the whites. Sometimes they own a spider, and generally a coffee pot and mill, which, as before, have been broken to use in the "buckra's house." They eat either directly out of the cooking instruments, or employ tin pans and cups, and (when they can afford it) thick-grained crockery painted with red flowers. They use their fingers or pocket-knives, steel forks, pewter spoons, and a worn-outtable-knife or two. Their food rarely includes more than hominy, corn-bread, rank fat bacon sides, coffee, and cheap molasses for breakfast. The coffee is without milk and sweetened by molasses. At dinner they have corn-bread, rice,—if thrifty,—pork "sides," and vegetables slimy with grease. At supper the same articles appear as at breakfast, minus the meat. On Sundays a plate of wheat bread, either biscuits or hoe-cake, is prepared for breakfast as a luxury, and what is left is warmed over for dinner and supper; and the coffee is rendered more palatable by a modicum of exceedingly coarse brown sugar. The gardens of the negroes contain only a few species of plants: sweet potatoes, Irish potatoes more rarely, peas, beans, water-melons, and collards, the last altogether preponderating. A family that can afford it keeps a pig impounded during the year, fattening it to kill at Christmas. But the negroes have yielded another proof of Macaulay's assertion that in every human being there is a tendency to ameliorate his condition. They are ambitious to increase the comforts of life, as well as to give leisure to their females and education to their children. Many of them have invested their earnings in a cow, and most of them rear fowls. But side by side with this tendency may often be descried the fatal disposition that has been the curse of Ireland: the desire, if I may so put it, to burrow in a hole. They will buy an acre or two, build a cottage, move in, and live in sloth and filthiness on what they can raise on their half-cultivated lot.

All the above remarks will apply with but few variations to the condition of the sand-hill whites, most of whom are inveterate beggars.

Since the war many ladies, both among the aristocrats and the respectable class, have been obliged to do their own cooking. In fact, one is esteemed fortunate to be able to employ a cook. The kitchens used to be detached from the dwelling-houses, and after being cooked the meals were brought across the yard to the dining-room. But this plan has fallen into desuetude, the ladies, not liking to bring dishes across the yard, cooking in some apartment of the dwelling-house. Stoves have come into universal use, something which was not the case when there were plenty of negroes to bend over the fire. Most ladies, too, have to be their own house-maids, sweeping out, dusting, and making the beds. The boys cut the wood, and the girls assist their mother. With such families, as a consequence, hospitality has been below par. When company arrives, the lady of the house is taken entirely aback. She is usually altogether prevented from sitting in the parlor, as she has either to cook or to set the table. Even if servants are employed she has to oversee them, as negroes never do anything without being told. The fare is nearly always homely and (owing to the unskillfulness of the amateur lady cook or the ignorance and coarseness of the negro cook) badly prepared. The crockery is not only cracked and old, but is odd. I used to ask—until I learned better—the lady of the house, when dining out, to pass me her plate (as of course families very generally wait on themselves) so that I could help her to some dish before me. "Oh, no," she would answer; "I won't trouble you; just hand me the dish, and I will help myself." Chance sometimes revealed the motive of her obstinacy. All the plates had been given to the guests and to the family (some of the latter, perhaps, taking soup-plates), while, concealed behind the tea-service, she was eating from a saucer. When one course (if, as is exceedingly infrequent, there is more than one) is finished, some member of the family, one of the boys, usually, will rise, clear the table, and put on the dessert.

Not only stoves but sewing-machines and other household utensils are much more common than before the war. The whites, having to do their own work, are clamorous for conveniences in which they would not indulge their slaves. It is proper to remark, however, that the negroes are usually rather too uncivilized to be trusted with labor-saving machines requiring any delicacy of management. Negro seamstresses always (except a few who were reared and trained in cultivated families) perform coarse sewing, and the washer-women, I might as well remark, badly damage the clothes they work on, iron-rusting them, tearing them, breaking off buttons, and burning them brown; and as for starch!—Colored cooks, too, generally abuse stoves, suffering them to get clogged with soot, and to "burn out" in half the time they ought to last.

It was for a time a rarity to see a new buggy or carriage, or a decent horse, in the State. The horses were spoiled for driving or riding by plow service, and the only vehicles were those preserved throughout the war. The carriages of the best-off citizens were lumbering, shabby, old, *ante-bellum* coaches, drawn by either two mules or a mule (with a shaved tail) and a regular Rozinante.[9] The harness would be patched, the whip worn down one half and turned into a handle for a leather lash. To a large extent this is yet the case, though at present many are able to keep a decent buggy; but new carriages are scarcely ever seen. In Columbia, however, the republican officials, white and colored, sport magnificent twenty-five-hundred-dollar turn-outs, with livery and blooded stock. In fact, at one time, it was thought a sure sign of dishonesty, by the whites of that city, for a man to dash about in a fine carriage or landaulet.

The homes of the negroes are dens of filth, giving off an intolerable stench. They were formerly compelled to devote some attention to cleanliness by their masters, but neglect it, now they are free. Their beds are clotted with dirt. Their domestic habits and relations are extremely barbarous, unsettled, and immoral. In consequence of their bad food and unhygienic conduct they are usually diseased to a lamentable degree. "How do you do, this morning?" To such an inquiry a colored person will never reply, "First rate." The invariable response is, "Well, I'm rather poorly," "I'm not so well, this morning," "I'm sorter middling, sir," or "I'm jes' betwixt and between." The whites ridicule this as affection, but really half of it is *not* put on. The rate of mortality among the negroes, both in cities and in the country, greatly exceeds that of the whites. Yet their constitutions must be wonderfully hardy to stand the strain they bear so well.

Dressing among the whites has been very plain. Threadbare garments, with holes at the elbows and shreds on the edges of the sleeves, have been quite common. Broadcloth has been so scarce as to excite a stare, and that, too, even in towns. Ladies thought themselves fortunate to get beyond calicoes. But for a year or so past a new era has been dawning. Broadcloth is often seen; ladies wear more costly outfits. The fashions of the North are, of course, imitated by the wealthy. Godey, Harper's Bazar, Demorest, Peterson, and Frank Leslie are very ordinarily subscribed to.[10] The dress of the negroes is simply disgusting; their clothes are stiff with mingled grease and dirt. It is unpleasant to have one of them approach within ten feet of you. They keep a tin basin at home in which they sometimes wash. But it is more customary to see them performing their ablutions in the horse trough, wiping their faces on their sleeves. During the summer they bathe in creeks, putting on their clothes while still wet. Their babies are kept in a horribly filthy condition.

The negro children in isolated places hardly ever wear more than a shirt, and it is not so startling a thing to see them playing about naked. Half the clothing of the negroes is begged from the whites, who give them cast-off garments nearly worn out. It is often impossible to discern the original piece of a coat or pair of pants, or its intended color, owing to the number of party-colored patches. They sometimes make suits out of gunny-bags. Their shoes are brogans or worn-out boots begged from the whites. The women wear turbans or go bare-headed. The negro men, as a general thing, did not wear hats before their emancipation. But they have since displayed quite a zeal to procure head wear, though not a few yet go uncovered. Negroes never bring their hats into white people's houses; they drop them on the steps or on the piazza or just inside the entry door, on the floor. They don't know (unless house servants) how to knock at doors. They will wait at the front gate an hour, till some one comes out to them, or rattle the gate or beat on it—or perhaps on the front steps—with their sticks (they all carry sticks), but will never come up the steps and knock.

Yet, so contradictory is human nature, notwithstanding what has been said, the negro is essentially a dandy, loving fine dress and decorations above all things. The females, particularly, are excessively fond of colors, and delight to parade on Sundays in the cast-away habiliments of their mistresses. The legislators and others in their higher society are first-class swells. Among women of pure African extraction a white man can never discover one really beautiful, although the males are sometimes undoubtedly handsome. But among the mulattoes, and especially those the most of whose blood is white, there are occasionally to be observed females who can lay claim to unmistakable beauty, and whose color adds all the more to their loveliness from recalling associations of the East.

Tobacco is used by nearly every man and boy in the South. Among the whites for a long time succeeding the war, pipes, being less expensive than cigars, were extensively in request. Cigars, though usually cheap ones, are now, however, in every-day use. The office-holding blacks are, of course, extensive consumers of such merchandise; indeed, they are about the only purchasers among us of the finest brands. The common negroes always beg the stumps of white men's cigars, and all their women smoke! The females among the sand-hillers also make use of the weed.

Every man, white or black, rich or poor, aristocrat or plebeian, keeps a gun or pistol. The whites are nearly always first-class marksmen. There is so much forest land in the State that a mile's walk from a city will conduct you to game, and of course those who live far from gay cities and the ways of men have much ampler facilities for hunting. Deer, though they are undoubtedly much thinned, are often found in the river swamps; foxes are often encountered, and wild turkeys, birds, squirrels, raccoons, opossums, and rabbits abound. Sporting is, therefore, universally popular. The negroes, when first permitted the handling of fire-arms, were as inferior to the whites in sharp-shooting as the Mohican chief in Cooper's novel was to the Deerslayer. Practice, however, has improved them; and the only limit to that with them is the expense. Every Southerner is also ambitious to own blooded stock, horses, dogs, hounds, and game fowls; want of means, though, has seriously interfered with the gratification of such tastes. Horse-racing and, to a less degree, cock-fighting are popular to excess. The negroes in their humble way imitate; they all own dogs, and frequently plume themselves on their fine roosters. The white is invariably a good, usually a graceful rider, and is fond of the exercise. The negro loves nothing better than to be allowed to mount on horseback, and is always a good rider, rarely a graceful one. White ladies used to be famous for their equestrian accomplishments, but, owing to the inferiority of all the horses in the country, they now seldom ride.

Circuses appear in this State only during the fall and winter. The fondness for them is, of course, universal, but is most ardent among the negroes and poor whites. They took in so much money from the former, year before last, that the legislature passed a law requiring all circuses to pay a license fee of one hundred dollars for every day they exhibit. Photographers perambulate the country occasionally, and meet with extensive patronage, especially from the negroes. Magic-lantern shows under canvas, minstrel companies and jugglers also reap a rich harvest among the sand-hillers and colored people. At circuses there are always placed two series of seats on opposite sides of the tent; the whites occupy one of these, the negroes the other. The clown and other performers invariably, unless their duties take them round, stay on the side nearest the whites, facing pointedly towards them, and never vouchsafing the colored folks a glance; and at these latter the clown never fails to throw jest after jest. The minstrels, too, always have jokes to make on the negroes and the republican party.

There are no first-class theatres in the State, and only three or four of an inferior description in Columbia and Charleston. Nevertheless, at the latter place the audiences at classic performances are highly intelligent and critical. Indeed, I doubt if an actor has a harder ordeal to undergo anywhere else in the United States except at Boston. Charlestonians rarely manifest their enthusiasm, and even when the playing is keenly relished the artists see but little to indicate that such is the case.

Negroes predominate in the crowds at cheap shows, circuses, and courts of justice, hangings, and so on. In all such gatherings each race contrives, by a process of elective affinity, to congregate by itself. Executions are yet public, and are never attended, even in the remotest county seat, by less than six or seven thousand people.[11] They are intensely demoralizing. When a negro, for instance, is to be hanged he usually has religious services in his cell daily for a week prior to the appointed time. These are opened to the public, and are thronged by those of his own race. On the scaffold prayers are made, which extract groans of assent from the concourse, frenzied by the speech of the usually repentant and confessing criminal. Hymns are then sung to wild airs, the colored spectators joining. A dead silence then ensues; this is broken by the falling of the drop, and as the doomed man is launched into eternity a piercing and universal shriek arises, the wildest religious mania seizes on the crowd, they surge to and fro, sing, and raise the holy dance. The scene is often shocking above description.

A strong taste for traveling is growing up among the whites. Before the war this was by no means so prevalent, or, at least, so noticeable. There are several watering-places and mineral springs in the State, which are every year numerously visited. The custom of journeying North is being resumed as rapidly as poverty will permit. I believe this taste was created by the late civil contest, which, by taking thousands of men to a distance from their homes, gave them a love for adventure and for seeing strange places. The example of the aristocrats before the war was not such as to encourage this disposition in the lower orders of society. They were, as a rule, self-content, and averse to going abroad—unless for a formal trip to finish off their education—where they would have to mix with strangers. It was, perhaps, a natural result of slavery. The younger members of the working class proper among the whites, together with the sand-hillers, form a vast majority who have never been above ten miles from home nor seen a locomotive.

Social life in Charleston is very peculiar so far as relates to the highest circles of society. The private residences are usually large and, though old-fashioned, convenient. They have numerous latticed balconies and are environed with ample yards, provokingly walled, in which the orange and other delicious fruits are propagated, or which are filled with rare and choice flowers. The houses, thus situated, have a delightful and indescribable air of retirement and comfort. They are owned mainly by wealthy planters on the neighboring seacoast and islands. Each of these, also, has usually a large-sized residence on his plantation, and there and in Charleston he and his family reside during alternate portions of the year. There the rice planters keep up their old customs as far as possible and form a nucleus about which Southern aristocracy may yet be restored.

Every year the Masons, Grangers, and other organizations hold sessions of their grand bodies in Charleston or Columbia; at the latter place there is also an annual state fair. On these occasions, as well as other celebrations, the railroads reduce their fares one half, and thousands of visitors throng the cities. Gayeties of this nature were at a discount for several years after the war, but are now fast reviving. Public entertainments, concerts, tableaux, county fairs, balls, etc., not to mention private parties and dances, have become as common as in normal times. Amateur base-ball clubs have sprung up everywhere. Public match games between Nines from a distance, which lead to dinners and picnics, are frequent. These things indicate the healing of the late wounds.

As usual, the negroes imitate. They are literally crazy about traveling. The railroad officials are continually importuned by them to run extra trains, excursion trains, and so on, on all sorts of occasions: holidays, picnics, Sunday-school celebrations, church dedications, funerals of their prominent men, circuses, public executions. The fare is generally, on all such excursions, reduced to fifty cents for the round trip from any point passed. They attract whole counties of negroes, and it is delightful to witness their childish wonder and enjoyment and behavior on the cars. The colored youth, too, have begun organizing base-ball clubs, which often challenge each other to match games. And hops and parties, though of course of a pretty uncouth kind, are frequent among the younger blacks of both sexes.

Thanksgiving Day is not considered or celebrated as a holiday by the whites, who keep on with their usual business. Slimly attended religious services are held, but no turkeys are killed. The negroes observe it to some extent in their churches and by picnics. Christmas is, however, indisputably *the* Southern holiday among all classes and conditions of men both white and colored. Easter and Good Friday were many years ago not very generally observed, except by the liturgical churches. They were esteemed too popish; now, however, they are rapidly increasing in favor with all denominations among the whites. The blacks, of course, know nothing about them. The whites altogether refrained from celebrating the Fourth of July up to the year before last, when, for the first time since the war, the military companies of Charleston and Columbia joined in Augusta, Georgia, with the similar bodies of that city in a commemoration of the day. But this year there was no attempt at all to observe it. The Centennial at Philadelphia awakened considerable interest in this State, from which it received many visitors. The negroes universally celebrate their emancipation on the Fourth of July instead of on the real anniversary.

It was a custom formerly to give the negroes several days of rest at Christmas time; and they still insist on the dispensation, which has become perpetual by prescription. The negro is a thorough believer in holidays, of which he takes a great number.

Excepting base-ball clubs the negroes have among themselves scarcely any social associations, if I may so term them, a fact which contrasts singularly with the zeal which they have evinced in connecting themselves with political and religious organizations. They have, perhaps, in the State about half a dozen local and languishing temperance societies. But the whites have rigorously shut them out from national orders like the Sons of Temperance, the Good Templars, the Knights of Pythias, the Odd Fellows, the Masons, and the Grangers. Nor have they had sufficient intelligence and energy to found such fraternities among themselves. The only exception to this is a branch of the Masonic brotherhood, which has a few sickly subordinate lodges and a state lodge; for this a charter was obtained, I am informed, from the state lodge of Massachusetts. These colored Masons are not recognized by the white lodges or grand body of the State.

The various orders which I mentioned above are favorite institutions among the whites. The Patrons of Husbandry, in particular, have a very flourishing organization. There are frequent reunions held of the survivors of old Confederate brigades and regiments, at which sentiments are usually expressed not precisely loyal to the Union. Among the females the Ladies' Memorial Associations enjoy much popularity. These are local in character, I believe; when feasible, they give dinners, concerts, fairs, and other entertainments for the purpose of raising money to build a public monument to the memory of Confederate soldiers buried in the vicinity. Scores of these monuments have already been erected. Addresses the very reverse of friendly to the national government are delivered on these occasions, as well as on Memorial Days, when the whole white population of a town turns out in procession, headed by the Ladies' Memorial Association, and decorates the graves. Poems, too, are commonly recited, either specially written for the occasion by local bards unknown to fame, or such "old, old stories" as Collins' ode, "How sleep the brave."[12]

There is also among the ladies an organization having for its object the construction of a monument to the memory of Calhoun. A year or so ago it was proposed to turn over the funds they had accumulated to the Ladies' Memorial Association, above described, to assist in the work of rearing monuments over the dead Confederates. The suggestion was approved by the newspapers, which said that were this "iron man" (as Miss Martineau called him) for a moment to awake he would sanction the idea.[13] In Charleston there is also a "Home," founded by popular contribution, for the impoverished widows and orphans of Confederate soldiers. This charitable institution has undoubtedly rendered much needed and meritorious service.

The colored people of all tints are regarded as negroes by the whites, and these mixed bloods associate with those of pure African extraction on terms of perfect equality. I have never encountered any cases where a mulatto put on airs, or was the subject of jealousy to a black on account of his white blood.[14]

My task is now done. But before closing I trust I shall be pardoned a little sentiment. The old plantation days are passed away, perhaps forever. My principles now lead me to abhor slavery and rejoice at its abolition. Yet sometimes in the midst of the heat and toil of the struggle for existence, the thought involuntarily steals over me that we have seen better days. I think of the wild rides after the fox and the deer; of the lolling, the book, the delicious nap, on the balcony, in the summer-house, or on the rustic seat on the lawn; of the long sittings at meals, and the after-dinner cigar; of the polished groups in easy but vivacious conversation in the parlor; of the chivalric devotion to beautiful women; of the pleasant evening drives; of the visits to the plantation, with its long, broad expanse of waving green, dotted here and there with groups of industrious slaves; of the long rows of negro cabins with little pickaninnies playing about them; of the old well with its beam and pole for drawing, and of the women with pails of water on their heads; of the wild old field airs ringing out from the cabins at night; of the "Christmas gif', Massa," breaking your slumbers on the holiday morn; of the gay devices for fooling the dignified old darkies on the first of April; of the faithful old nurse who brought you through infancy, under whose humble roof you delighted to partake of an occasional meal; of the flattering, foot-scraping, clownish, knowing rascal to whom you tossed a silver piece when he brought you your boots; of the little darkies who scrambled for the rind after you had eaten your water-melon on the piazza in the afternoon, —and, "as fond recollection presents them to view," I feel the intrusive swelling of the tear of regret. And so it is with every Southerner; tears rise in his heart and gather to his eyes as he thinks of the days that are no more. The Southerners of old used to be perhaps the happiest of men. There was nothing to disturb them, nothing to do, nothing they wished done that others were not at hand to do. Happiness was not only their being's end and aim, but its enjoyment their one occupation. Now the cares of life, the struggle for a living, weigh them down. It often strikes me, as I think of the intense enjoyment of the olden time, that perhaps just as the strongest force in physics is evolved from the greatest consumption of material, so it is ordained in human affairs that the most exquisite happiness shall be founded on the intensest misery of others.

*A South Carolinian.*

# The Result in South Carolina
*The Atlantic Monthly* 41, no. 243 (January 1878)

In South Carolina there are five very noticeable results of the president's policy: first, the decreased expense of the state government, and its increased purity and efficiency; secondly, a great decrease of crime and disorder, a marked increase of material prosperity, and a striking renewal of public, social, and military spirit among the whites; thirdly, the utter extinction of the republican party, and a revival of the old political intolerance; fourthly, a renewal of interest in federal affairs on the part of the whites; and lastly, the banishment of the negro from politics, and his enhanced material prosperity.

But in order to understand what may be said on these points, it is requisite to take a glance at the condition of the State when the policy in question was adopted.

During the canvass of 1876 the democrats openly announced that they purposed to carry the election, peaceably if possible but forcibly if necessary. They threatened that if Chamberlain should win, they would refuse to pay taxes to his government. When it was ascertained that the votes actually cast gave Hampton about eleven hundred majority, their indignation at the idea of going behind the returns was exceeded only by their indignation that the electoral returns at Washington were not subjected to the process; they unanimously declared that they would have Hampton or a military government. Their deliberate design all along was to achieve a party victory if they could, and a revolution if they could not. Their arming, their martial organization, their violent proceedings during the campaign, and the responsive excesses of the negroes when aroused have become matters of history. When President Hayes was inaugurated, the State was in anarchy. Within a month after the election the garrisons which had been stationed by Grant and Chamberlain in nearly every populated place in the State had been withdrawn from all points except Columbia, Charleston, and Greenville, where garrisons ordinarily are posted. After their withdrawal the hostile races confronted each other. The violent passions of the campaign not only did not cool, but became inflamed by the establishment of rival state governments. These governments, headed respectively by Chamberlain and Hampton, had each its set of officials in every county and in every town. Nothing but the fear of resistance in each particular case kept the blacks from lawlessness towards the whites. Nothing but dread of the torch, solicitude for their families, and party policy, the wish to do themselves and Tilden no harm in the North, restrained the whites from ruthlessly putting down the blacks. Wherever immunity seemed possible the negroes were burning the buildings of whites,[1] stealing their property, and assembling as militia or in mobs to assail whites and terrorize communities by riot and tumult; while murders of whites during arsons, burglaries, highway robberies, and riots became frequent. Every white family in the country kept watch at night, or slept in dread, with dogs turned loose in the yard and the gun at the bedside. Every village and town was patrolled by relays of white citizens from dark till daylight. The moment a crime was reported, the mounted rifle clubs assembled from all parts and scoured the country, to the terror of the blacks, arresting suspected criminals, conveying them to jail, or inflicting summary vengeance. They were sometimes resisted by the colored militia, and regular battles occurred. Individual

*Governor Chamberlain being sworn into office by Probate Judge Boone in the House of Representatives, December 7, 1876. From Frank Leslie's Illustrated Newspaper, December 30, 1876. Image courtesy of the South Caroliniana Library, University of South Carolina, Columbia.*

members of the races were constantly quarrelling and fighting. The courts, though recognized by both parties, vainly tried to execute justice. Blacks on the juries would consent to no conviction of one of their race prosecuted by a white man. White jurymen acted similarly in the cases of whites indicted for violence towards blacks. The rival officials in each county were endeavoring *vi et armis* to oust their opponents from the court-houses, or to assert their authority over the people. They were backed up, respectively, by the whites and blacks, and collisions were happening every day. A reign of terror existed. Trade was paralyzed. The merchants' stocks grew small and were not replenished. Men with money were afraid to lend or invest. The farmers delayed their operations. Such was the ordeal to which the whites subjected themselves rather than submit. They swore they could be overcome only when twenty thousand federal troops should be sent to the State, and kept there; when they should be relentlessly crushed by the bayonet, disarmed, their prominent men punished, and every deputy of a Chamberlain sheriff supported by a posse of blue coats whenever he went to arrest a white man, or sell property for taxes.

*The inauguration of General Wade Hampton as Governor, December 14, 1876. From Frank Leslie's Illustrated Newspaper, December 30, 1876. Image courtesy of the South Caroliniana Library, University of South Carolina, Columbia.*

This state of things continued till April. But the negroes were gradually yielding. The long-hoped for recognition from Washington did not come. The depression of the times began to affect them. They had spent the earnings of the previous year, and they had stolen all the property they dared. Hundreds were being thrown into jail to await trial at the courts, which meet but once in four months. Starvation was at their doors. The spring was coming on, and they could secure no advances from the merchants to plant their crops; while the white farmers feared to enter into arrangements with laborers till they could see ahead. The Hampton government, also, with admirable management, gradually pushed the opposition to the wall. The courts and the tax payers were on its side: the former recognized its legitimacy, and the latter voluntarily contributed funds for its expenses; while the Chamberlain government was adjudged illegal, and could raise no supplies. At length the whole machinery of the government was in the possession of the democracy. Its authority was, indeed, denied by more than half the citizens, but its processes were everywhere enforced; while the authority of the other faction obtained nowhere but within the granite walls of the state-house, which inclosed a garrison of twenty-two soldiers of the United States.

Towards the end of March Chamberlain and Hampton, by invitation of the president, visited Washington to confer with him as to the condition of South Carolina. The result is known. Orders were issued for the withdrawal of the troops from the state-house. Chamberlain at once returned to South Carolina, and knowing that further resistance was useless soon surrendered the executive office, first publishing an address, bitterly commenting on the action of the president. Hampton immediately took possession, and has since been undisputed governor of the State.

The whites hardly knew what to say at first. Their strongest passions had been aroused during the contest. They had staked everything upon the issue. During the dual months they had hung on to the hope that Tilden would be seated, and that then would come relief, victory, and revenge. But the inauguration of Hayes crushed every expectation. Nothing was to be looked forward to then, they thought, but a continuation of their distractions. Chamberlain's government would be recognized by the president. They were determined to repudiate it. The lower house of Congress might refuse the means to prop it up with the army; but they dared not crush it out and assert their supremacy over the blacks, for fear that a revulsion of popular feeling in the North would force Congress to take action against them; and while it lasted, lawlessness and material depression were inevitable. During March the despondency of the whites was inexpressible. They became willing to agree to almost any terms which would rid them of Chamberlain and negro rule, and give them "Hampton and home government." It gradually dawned on them that relief was coming from the president whom they had expected to prolong their troubles. When the final announcement came, their joy was bewildering. Grand demonstrations, the firing of cannon, the ringing of bells, greeted Hampton on his return along the roads, at Columbia, and at Charleston. A sense of relief at once pervaded the community. Trade forthwith revived. The lean shelves of the merchants were soon filled with goods. Securities rose in price. Credit was re-established. The farmers, white and colored, secured advances for the year, and went heartily to work. Thousands of colored men, long idle, obtained employment. Race conflicts ceased, and the decrease of crime was tremendous. The negroes had been losing hope, were starving and exhausted, and, glad to have the suspense terminated in whatever way, submitted quietly. Hampton's tact contributed to the result. He gave a public reception in the city hall to the colored citizens of Charleston, shook several thousand by the hand, made them a stirring speech, promising that their rights as citizens should be maintained, and called on them and the whites alike to drop enmity, resume amicable relations, and go to work to build up private and public welfare. The colored militia officers waited on him, were recognized as officers, and promised that their organization should be respected and continued.

We are now prepared to consider the outgrowths of the president's action. As stated at the outset, the first is general improvement in the workings of our government; and that even when compared with the administration of Governor Chamberlain, who was hampered by the party which had elected him, and from whose members, though they were mostly corrupt or willing to be corrupted, he was expected generally to select his subordinates. The new government was set in operation by the ejection of the republican comptroller-general, treasurer, and other state officers from their offices in the state-house. They had been elected on the *prima-facie* vote, like Hampton himself; but the democratic candidates made contest on technicalities before the supreme court. Pending the decision, Hampton arbitrarily and very unexpectedly closed the offices on the incumbents. Records were probably thereby preserved from destruction which have since given weighty evidence against the reconstruction corruptionists. The ever ready supreme court soon installed the Hampton claimants. The governor next convened the legislature, which met on April 24th. This was because we had had no tax levy or other legislation during the winter, on account of the dispute over the organization of the legislature. The senate, which had been recognized as legal by both parties, was republican by three or four votes. The returns had made the house democratic. But a sufficient number of democrats had been rejected (without seating their opponents, the election being pronounced null and void from fraud) by the returning board, or, as it is called here, the board of state canvassers, to give the republicans a majority. The democrats thus counted out, however, were declared by the supreme court to be entitled to their seats, and accordingly had claimed them when the general assembly met in December. They had then been excluded from the state-house by the aid of federal soldiers. Thereupon, they and the other democratic members adjourned to a public hall in the city, and organizing declared themselves the legal house. The republican members remained in the state-house. They did not have a majority of that number of members of which the house should consist, but they claimed a quorum because they had a majority of all declared elected by the canvassing board, and they also asserted themselves to be the true house. They were called to order by the clerk of the last house, and recognized, on a strict party vote, by the senate, which afterwards united with them and Governor Chamberlain in enacting laws which could never be executed. The democratic senators protested, but did not secede.[2] The democratic house was adjudicated legal, as usual, by the supreme court, but did not try to legislate, merely joining with the democratic senators to inaugurate Hampton and elect Butler, as described below. Both houses and the senate had adjourned before the new year. Under Hampton's call the senate and the democratic house assembled as the legislature. The original members of the republican house, which had been swollen by admitting some republicans contesting the seats of democrats, now recognized the legality of this democratic house and applied for their seats. Only about half were admitted, and then only on condition of purging themselves at the bar of their contempt in joining the rival body, or, as most of them called it, "axing" pardon. The others were excluded upon the ground of fraud or of insufferable deportment. The new lieutenant-governor, on taking the chair of the senate, ordered several democrats claiming seats, but whose election was not conceded by the senate, to be sworn in; and by refusing to submit the matter to the senate, when the republican members appealed against his action, succeeded in so increasing the democratic minority that that party soon had practical control of the chamber.

Expenditures were greatly reduced by the new legislature. The salaries in 1876, under Chamberlain, amounted to $264,418; legislative expenses, $142,135; printing, $78,187. The appropriations under Hampton for 1877, for the same purposes, are: for salaries, $143,000; legislative expenses, $105,000; printing, $10,000. The total tax levy for 1876 was about thirteen mills on the dollar. This year (1877) it is ten mills, and would be smaller but for deficiencies for the preceding fiscal year. The cutting off of three mills means the reduction of the annual taxes by about $350,000. Local township taxation for schools is also abolished. This leads me to say that the appropriation this year for educational purposes ($100,000) is only about a third of what it used to be under republican rule, when, however, the most of it was stolen or wasted. The poll-tax is devoted to education by the constitution. Legislative corruption has ceased; and in every branch of the government, from the state and county administrations down to the courts of the peace justices, there is greatly increased efficiency. The appointees are men of intelligence and high standing, and are above temptation. So, also, are those elected. Four or five democrats in the senate, by voting with the republican senators in the spring, prevented for a while a reduction in legislative compensation. But the public raised such a storm that they had to recede and consent.

As a second result, not only have the unusual violence and infamous crimes of the fall and winter ceased, but the State is quieter, with less violation of law, than at any other time since the war. Further on, some circumstances will be noted which will contribute to explain these facts. The crops, by reason of hearty work and unwonted security, have been unusually good this year. The fall trade is brisker than since 1860. Every wholesale house in Charleston, and I suspect in the North, will attest this, and in the villages I have visited not only have merchants laid in larger stocks than is their custom, but many new stores have arisen. The railroads are doing well, and every branch of industry seems to be thriving. The taxes have ceased to be so great a burden, and it is probable that the unblushing repudiation, or, as it was called, scaling, of the legislature in 1873 so cut down the iniquitous bonded debt that it amounts to but four or five millions. A commission is investigating the condition of this debt, which has long been in confusion. But the revival of spirit amongst the whites, long cast down by vicissitude, poverty, and the *post-bellum* troubles, has been remarkable. Long excluded from office, they have devoted themselves to work, and while looking on the government with sullen or malignant hostility have manifested little curiosity about its workings. Now everybody is a candidate for position, and everybody is discussing everything about our rulers and politics. The ladies, after an intermission of ten years, grace the sessions of the legislature by their presence. Newspapers have increased their circulation and new ones have been established. Charleston, which could long support but one daily, now boasts of two. County towns, where one weekly with a "patent outside" found it hard to keep from starving, now sustain two and even three weeklies, printed on both sides at home.[3]

The gayeties of the summer have rivaled those of *ante-bellum* times. There has been no end of visiting and hospitality, traveling and attendance on watering-places, parties, balls, public entertainments, etc. Associations have been well attended. The agricultural and horticultural fairs for the year have been, and promise to continue, unexampled successes. The governor, through the adjutant-general, was authorized by law to organize the whites into a militia, to be distinct from the negro national guard; and the adjutant-general's office has had more business than any other at the capital. Innumerable companies have been formed and organized into the higher divisions; and the enthusiasm over titles, uniforms, drilling, parades, military hops, and so on, has been tremendous. In all these things the old aristocracy, as usual, takes the lead.

Republicanism is dead, and the old intolerance has revived. No overt violence has been offered to any one on account of his republican sentiments since Hampton's triumph, though there has been plenty of hooting and gibing.[4] But it is because the republicans have kept very quiet. There is no federal support now, and they know from the experience of the autumn what would follow if a vigorous party course were adopted, calculated to consolidate the negro vote and win: that is, violence and starvation. Furthermore, the democrats have shown themselves willing to use the election machinery, now in their hands, to achieve victory, and did so as flagrantly in the first elections under Hampton as the republicans in their prime. The latter see that it would be of no use to gain votes. Negroes, too, dependent on whites, and consequently the majority, are now made to understand that to cast a republican ticket means discharge, prescription, and starvation. Therefore, perceiving in what corner the wind sits, perhaps a third of the colored men now profess democracy, and vote in accordance, to the great joy and satisfaction of their employers or patrons. You can see advertisements before the shops of negroes, like this: "Patronize So and So, the only colored democratic barber [or shoemaker] in town." These converts would have been summarily bulldozed by their sable brethren up to this year, but the whites now delight in protecting and petting them. Since Chamberlain's retirement there have been fifteen or twenty elections in single counties at different times, to fill vacancies in the legislature, etc. On such occasions great numbers of young white men, largely from adjacent counties, ride to and remain about the polls, "to see fair play," they explain. These have not attempted openly to molest, but they have certainly frightened the republican negroes. Accordingly, *every election* has gone democratic. The republicans put up tickets only two or three times at first, but never think of it now. Even Charleston, Darlington, and Orangeburg, the old strongholds of radicalism, have gone democratic with no opposition, except in the last. The republicans meet in few places now; their organization has fallen to pieces. But the democrats preserve strict party discipline. Some candidates, defeated before their conventions, have threatened to bolt, and the republicans have offered to vote for such; but thereupon such a cry was raised, not only in the county but all over the State, that no such bolt has happened yet, or is likely to.

The republicans have furthermore lost their leaders. The whites regard the negro as an inferior animal, admirably adapted to work and to wait, and look on him, "in his proper place," with a curious mixture of amusement, contempt, and affection. It is when he aspires to participate in politics or otherwise claim privileges that their hatred becomes intense. They knew that the main body of blacks were ignorant and by themselves harmless; that they had been following politicians, and would readily resume work and give no more trouble. Consequently, there was little desire to persecute them after the settlement. Not so with the leaders, however. There has been a relentless determination to purge the offices of republicans, to get rid of every vestige of the hateful carpet-bag *régime*, and to bring its upholders to a heavy reckoning. Nor have there been wanting reasons or plausible pretexts. The republican representatives elect[ed] from Charleston County, seventeen in number, were refused seats in the lower house, the election being annulled on the ground of fraud, and a new one ordered. This would have been proper enough had not the delegates from Edgefield been seated and lionized. The colored justice of the supreme court has been impeached for drunkenness.[5] A circuit judge, still too republican, was unseated by a technical objection to the way in which he had qualified the year before; and the legislature took some steps, and will probably complete them this winter, to declare vacant the seats of all the circuit judges, most of whom, despite their eminent services last fall, were once, in some way, mixed with republicanism, on account of a slight informality in the method of their election by the legislature in 1875. It was with difficulty, and only after bitter quarreling in caucus, that Hampton could induce the legislature to elect the facile white associate justice of the supreme court to the place of Chief-Justice Moses, on the latter's decease, in reward for indispensable services during the dual imbroglio.[6] I have referred to the treatment of the state treasurer, etc. A republican state attorney has been ousted,—for being a congressman at the same time. Half the republicans elected to county offices last November [1876] were unable to get bondsmen, so strong was the feeling; and many who did get them, have since had them to withdraw. So, new elections have been held and democrats put in.

But the most potent instrument for both purging and revenge has been prosecution for official misconduct. A legislative investigating committee has been sitting in Columbia since June, taking testimony and overhauling the state archives. In most of the counties, too, the grand juries have been examining witnesses and searching the records in the court-houses. Indictments and presentments without number have followed; and starting with two congressmen (a senator and a representative), passing by two ex-governors, several lieutenant-governors and speakers of the house, two ex-treasurers, two ex-comptroller-generals, and over half the republican members and ex-members of the legislature, with the ex-clerks, and coming down to numberless state attorneys and ex-state attorneys, county officers and ex-county officers,—treasurers, auditors, county commissioners, school commissioners, sheriffs, clerks of court, trial justices, school trustees and teachers,—we find that nearly all the republicans in the State who have ever held office are under indictment, are already convicted and punished, or have fled from justice.[7] So palpable is their guilt, generally, that even the most radical negroes on the juries are compelled to find true bills or verdicts of guilty. I should state that rumors are afloat that all the prominent parties under indictment in Columbia will not be prosecuted further should public opinion in the North condemn the proceeding. It is also proper to say that many rogues have had the case against them "nol. pros'd," upon condition of making restitution of their plunder to the State or of immediately resigning important offices which their prosecutors were desirous of getting. There have been no trials of cases worked up by the committee yet. It is notorious both in Columbia and the counties that not a few white democrats being implicated in some of the corruptions, their investigation has been promptly dropped to shield these democrats. The legislative committee has been compared to the Star-Chamber, sitting with closed doors and enjoining silence on all called before it. But there has been no lack of purely republican rascality to punish. Members of former legislatures, some still sitting, are indicted for taking bribes. A United States senator, individuals and members of rings and corporations, are indicted for bribing them. It has been discovered that a clerk of the senate issued thousands upon thousands of dollars in pay certificates to merchants, which although recorded as paid for stationery were really given for fine wines, liquors, cigars, furniture, novels, etc., for the private use of himself and certain senators. The managers of a colored state orphan asylum in Columbia, where were kept fifty poorly cherished children, are found to have been ordering for their wards, if the books may be trusted, hundreds of dollars' worth of assorted candies, whisky, water-melons, and carpets. A voucher was found in the comptroller-general's office for $4320 in figures. Being traced back it is seen that the original bill was for $320, and that the prefixing of the figure four has netted the forger as many thousand dollars. Another bill for $1100 in figures is metamorphosed by two neat additions to the ones into $4400. There are charges of frauds in issuing state bonds and funding coupons; for diverting the taxes to objects for which they had not been appropriated, etc. In the counties there are indictments for issuing and paying innumerable fraudulent claims on the county treasury, for defalcations and other crimes too numerous to mention. In one county the auditor and treasurer, who respectively assess and collect taxes, as a check upon each other, are found to have been in collusion, and to have doctored the books in their respective offices so as to leave unentered the taxes due and paid on large amounts of property, and to have pocketed the taxes thus unrecorded. Most, though by no means all, of the offenses in both state and county governments seem to have occurred prior to Governor Chamberlain's administration; that he strove to stem the corruption while chief executive everything goes to prove.

But prosecution is not confined to official malfeasance. In one county twenty or thirty prominent republicans are charged with perjury. The county went republican, but the officers elect could get no democrats to go on their bonds. No republicans were worth enough to stand, as the state laws require sureties to swear before a notary (false swearing being made perjury by statute) that they are worth the amount they stand for over and above their homestead ($1500) and debts; and yet the culprits in question took the required oaths and went on their friends' bonds, to be discovered and presented by a grand jury this spring. A colored legislator is among them. Another colored legislator has been sent to the penitentiary for bigamy. Others are in straits about fraudulent breaches of private trusts. When the legislature comes together again in December, it is possible that not a dozen republicans will be left in it.

But not only has there been a crusade against the politicians; there has been a relentless effort to bring to retribution and get out of the way all those negroes who, without holding office, made themselves obnoxious or dangerous, through vindictiveness or crime, to the whites. And this movement has been more formidable, or at least it has aroused far more excitement in the State, than the former. No whites have been prosecuted in the state courts for the violent crimes of the campaign; and when the Ellenton rioters were tried before the United States circuit court at Charleston, in June, the chief-justice presiding, the whites on the jury obstinately declined to find a verdict against them, and a mistrial was ordered. But hundreds upon hundreds of negroes, accused of participation in the arsons, the burglaries, the larcenies, the riots, and the murders of the republican rule, and especially of the last canvass and the dual months, have been and are now being prosecuted in the state courts, by the instigation of either grand juries or individuals. Civil business is rarely reached, so crowded is the criminal side of the courts; and even on the criminal side the docket is rarely cleared or a jail delivery made. The jails have been overcrowded all the year; a small one in the country, I have had occasion to notice, used to contain on an average about fifteen prisoners; there are now fifty-one in it, and it has the odor of a wild beast's cage in a managerie [*sic*]. The number of convicts in the penitentiary has increased from three hundred and fifty during the last year to nearly six hundred. Imprisonment is for longer terms, and as many as two and three negroes are frequently hung at a time, once (in May, I think) even five. The state constabulary, an oppressive instrument of republican invention, designed for use against the Ku-Klux Klan especially but the whites generally, has been turned against its inventors. These constables are appointed by a chief constable, who is named by the governor and senate. They exercise all the common law powers of constables and sheriffs, but are besides invested with detective duties, and have power to arrest without a warrant. In some counties, Darlington especially, where there was considerable lawlessness, the colored people have lived in terror of these officers. They have searched the houses of negroes freely, arrested right and left, often on suspicion, and acted with stringency in binding, knocking down, and even shooting stubborn prisoners. When they "go scouting," as they call it, they usually summon a posse of fifteen or twenty mounted white riflemen, and with them go scouring through the country, which has at times, from the frequency of such scenes, presented quite a military appearance. These posses are generally requisite, as the criminals have been numerous and desperate, resisting arrest, and sometimes inducing the negro population to aid them.

The guilt of most of the negroes prosecuted as described is so apparent on trial that it is impossible for a juror mindful of his oath to say otherwise than guilty. Yet there is a political aspect to the prosecutions, the crimes having been mostly the outgrowths of political disturbance, of which both whites and blacks are conscious. I should add, too, that there was much distress during the dual months, owing to the discharge and proscription of colored republican voters, many of whom were compelled by want to resort to crime, or to change their localities in order to get work. The odium, too, against a "loud-mouthed" or villainous negro is so great that white juries are in the habit of convicting him even when his innocence is clearly established, excusing themselves by saying that if not guilty in that instance, he has done other and worse things, is a bad egg, anyhow, and ought to be got rid of while the chance offers. This spirit has tempted many base whites to carry very worthy and blameless colored men into court on flimsy charges, and convictions are generally certain. But a good negro, quiet and hard-working, usually has white friends who, if he be maliciously indicted, will take up his quarrel, lending him money and influence, and testifying to his good character. Such negroes obtain very fair trials; and if convicted on some old, raked-up charge, and there be any ground, a petition is drawn up, influential signatures are secured, and a light sentence or pardon is often obtained.

Whatever names parties may hereafter bear in South Carolina, whatever local issues may divide them, or whatever may be their assumed general principles, one thing may safely be predicted: the whites, in the future as in the past, will not tolerate, unless forced, any party which aggressively and in real earnest advocates negro rights, or in the same manner denounces the past course of the South.

The whites were long so engrossed with home troubles as to care little for national affairs. In the ascendant again at home, they are now looking with no little interest at federal politics. They have returned to power like the Bourbons in having forgotten nothing, but unlike them in having learned something.[8] They have not forgotten the old issues and the struggle with the North. Nor have they ceased to think that this is a white man's government, and that the negro should keep his place. But they *have* learned, what once they did not seem to know, that they cannot always have their way. They have learned that separation from the Union is a thing attended with difficulty and danger of such magnitude that nothing hereafter, except the absolute certainty of success at small cost and unattended by risk of invasion, could induce a secession. Consequently, separation is rarely spoken of, and when spoken of is dismissed with a sigh or a laugh as something which, however desirable once, is now out of the question.

Nevertheless, Southerners look upon their connection with the Union as somewhat resembling the connection of Ireland with England;[9] as a thing forced and inevitable, and possibly not unbearable if they are allowed to rule at home; but at the bottom a distasteful subjection of one nation that has a right to be independent to another nation that has proved itself stronger in war. The expression of Mr. Key, "erring brethren," was promptly taken up and indignantly repudiated by every paper in the South.[10] The South will never admit that she was wrong in the issues that led to the war, or that her conquest was right.

The remarks of President Hayes during his recent tour South, that he recognized the Southerners as men who had fought for what they conscientiously believed right, and who had succumbed only before superior numbers, were enthusiastically received and quoted all over the South. Zeal for the Confederacy and rank in the Confederate army are every day flaunted in the papers or before the conventions as the highest possible recommendations of candidates for office. There is a very significant reluctance amongst the white military to march or parade under the United States flag; it is rarely done, and causes much aspersion from the spectators, state banners being used. This is not surprising when three fourths of Southern tradition relate to the war, and when every family has a Life of Lee or Jackson on the centre-table, and their portraits on the wall. But secession being impossible, everybody is full of suggestions as to how we should make the most of our situation in the Union. Some hope we can in the future elect a Southern president, gain the control of both houses of Congress, and then get everything possible out of the Union in the shape of offices, internal improvements, war losses, it may be, or more Southern States from Mexico and Spain, or by dividing Texas into four or five States, so as to acquire more votes in the senate. Many of these things are expected during the present administration. Others, however, are not so sanguine. The consciousness of the infrangible solidity of the South, joined to the hope of some democratic votes in the North, or of divisions in the republican party, encourage all to hope that the South will be able to make a more or less good showing for herself in the future. All are aware of the jealousy with which the action of a solid South will be watched at the North, and of the improbability of securing enough votes there to carry out a rabid sectional course. Consequently, they are likely to act with moderation, undertaking nothing until they have carefully ascertained its practicability. They will probably claim the management of the national democratic party; though there is another possibility: the antipathy to the Union, joined to the constrained acceptance of the last constitutional amendments (which makes but little difference now between democratic and republican platforms),[11] may cause the South hereafter to look on Northern democrats and Northern republicans with very much the same kind of feeling,—a feeling compounded half of aversion and half of eagerness to get all out of them that is possible.

It is not impossible that the South may essay a professedly conservative and independent, but really experimental and speculating course, joining sometimes with the Northern democrats and sometimes with the republicans, as it advantages most.

To sum up, the South is awake to the situation, but has settled on no policy for the future, and will be rabid or moderate as prudence dictates; there is no course too strange for her to adopt. If her solidity be broken, it will be on issues not relating to the war and the negro; or if on those issues, it will be because there is disagreement as to what lengths principles common to all should be carried. I should add that at present Southerners are very enthusiastic about the president, and grateful for his action. He might have protracted their sufferings. Their idea is that of late years the North has been swayed by fanatics, demagogues, and speculators; and there is immense relief to think that practical, conservative, and cultured men from a better element have come to the front. Many Southern leaders, emulous of Key, are becoming very ambitious of playing a part in national affairs, some even aspiring to the presidency. These affect a very conciliatory tone to attract Northern support.

But enough for the whites. Let us turn to the other color. Only three negroes have been killed by whites since March, and there has been a marked decrease of beatings and affrays. One reason is that the negroes, to use a popular phrase, are "lying low." Another is that violence towards negroes who do aggrieve whites is at present discouraged as impolitic, and redress is sought through the courts. When Chamberlain fell, the negroes were generally submissive; but many were moody and apprehensive for their liberty. They soon perceived that things went on with them just about the same under democratic as under republican rule. Their politicians lost office; but the change did not affect the main body, whose only connection with politics had been to vote once a year or so, and attend the occasional meetings of the party. The party was now broken up, and though still at liberty to vote they must be cautious in so doing not to offend their employers or patrons. They had long ago found that party and suffrage did them no appreciable good,—they had to work for a living all the same,—and only valued them because they were thought essential to keep down the democrats, who would of course restore slavery should they triumph. But the democrats were in at last; the persons of freemen were unmolested, their property secure. The brisker times soon began to increase their individual prosperity; and it is positively a fact that if a plebiscitum could be held in South Carolina to-morrow, it is questionable whether negro votes would not defeat the republicans. The prosecutions for political and personal crimes before mentioned have caused a renewal of apprehension at times and places. But it is discerned that the hard-working, respectable, quiet class of negroes are safe, and that only the leaders in the past iniquity and the evil spirits are in danger. Accordingly, they turn to work with renewed ardor, and strive to avoid offense and to placate the whites by settling up their liens and other debts, by frowning down pilfering, by courteous demeanor, or by a change in politics. It is amusing to hear how many of them voted for Hampton. This has led to a renewal of many kindly relations long severed. Whites are seen attending the funerals of their servants, aiding black children in their yards to learn by heart their "speeches" for the Sunday-school celebrations, or the girls to dress, and even taking peeps at colored festivities; while the negroes are again surrounding every white gathering.

In some localities, however, the arrest and carrying to prison of the negro leaders, known and perhaps loved by all, has caused great alarm and sorrow. Crowds bid them farewell at the railway stations, wring their pinioned hands, ask what is the difference between this and the old slave-traders' doings, and as the train moves off utter loud lamentations and raise wild hymns; even rescues have been attempted. The prevalence of larceny, bigamy, and the like, now and in the past, causes thousands of negroes to fear that their turn will come. Many have become either very moody and desperate or very obsequious. There has been an immense crop of offers to turn State's evidence. Negro jurors are often quite as ready now to convict those of their color prosecuted by whites as white jurors themselves. These things have resulted in the tremendous falling off of crime, before recounted, as crime in previous years has been comparatively safe, from the determination of the negroes, not to tell on or convict each other. Many negroes were so uneasy during the spring and summer that a proposition to emigrate to Liberia created great interest. Organization was attempted, but want of money has been in the way, as well as want of unanimity. So nothing, or little at least, is likely to come of it.[12]

The position of the whites towards the negro is just this: reënslavement is not desired by one in fifty, and is looked on as utterly impracticable, visionary, and dangerous, many even admitting that slavery in the past was an economical blunder. But they would not be unwilling to restrict the freedom of the negro in many such things as wandering about at night, holding public meetings, attending day schools,—or any at all,—and living in idleness; and to make the law stringent on him as regards contracts made with whites, or crimes committed against them. Nor is the idea of negro citizenship yet palatable. But some decency is to be expected in view of the platforms and pledges of the past few years, guaranteeing colored rights;[13] nor has the fear of Northern interference yet subsided. Consequently, while we are in the Union, encroachments on negro liberty will be made cautiously, slowly, and under disguises. But even already, in this State, there are indications of what the feeling is. The new legislature made it a criminal offense to sell or buy seed cotton at night, there having been much stealing of the staple from the field at night by negroes in the past; and decreed that convicts in the penitentiary should hereafter be farmed out to contractors for labor on railroads, etc. The whites everywhere applauded both measures, particularly the last, on account of their race significance, while the negroes everywhere deplored them for the same reason. Few or, in many cases, no negro jurymen were summoned in over half the counties in the State for the fall courts, the panels being for the most part white; while many papers, and in several counties (Abbeville, for instance) the grand juries, have recommended the whipping-post, to which harsh memories will cling, as a punishment for larceny; and many grand juries and all the papers are advocating constitutional enactments disfranchising voters who fail to pay their capitation or other tax, or who are convicted of larceny, and prescribing an educational qualification for voting and jury duty. This reminds me that the colored university was relentlessly broken up, an appropriation being refused to pay even the arrears of the professors. It was very odious to the whites from its perversion, having once been to the old, gentlemanly, chivalric Palmetto element as Oxford to the tories and the churchmen. The legislature has resolved to turn it into a white college again, and give the negroes a college for themselves, with an equal pecuniary support.[14] There is great prejudice in this State against free schools for any color; nor have the airs put on by colored school children contributed to remove it. Policy, however, and past promises will probably impel the maintenance of a free-school system for some time at least, but on a less extensive scale. It is proper to add that some cultured Southerners are in favor of educating and elevating the negro as the best way to solve our race difficulties. But it is doubtful if their views will prevail against inherited prejudice.

Reconstruction has certainly failed to make the negro a full-fledged citizen, with all the rights and privileges enjoyed by the white race. But no longer a slave, owning perhaps a tenth of the property in the State, free to earn money and to go where and hire to whom he pleases, with his rights of property and (while he votes with his master, or refrains from voting) his person secure, he certainly has made an immense stride forward from the time of the overseer and the patrol, the quarter and the plantation; nay, even from the time when he was set free, penniless and helpless, despised and ridden over by his former masters, and the prey of greedy adventurers from the North. As to the future, he is side by side with a branch of that race which has yet found no superior on the earth; and the evolutionists should watch with interest that which will prove to be a most instructive phase in the progress of the great struggle for existence.

Readers of this paper may find themselves left in some doubt as to the sentiments of the author on the policy whose results are recounted. Nor should they be charged with a lack of discernment. Over the first and second results stated, the author is inclined on the whole to rejoice. In the third, fourth, and fifth results described, while he finds some things to approve, he perceives much to deplore. Consequently, he knows not what to say at present. His mind is not made up.

*A South Carolinian.*

# Wild with All Regret:
# A Tale of Reconstruction

From *Plantation Lays and Other Poems* / Columbia, S.C.: C.A. Calvo, Jr., 1884

I'll not invoke the Muses,
  But with a sheriffs sale,
A very homely matter,
  You may think, will start my tale.
Yet there is not a subject
  You can find in all romance
More tragic than the auction
  Of an old inheritance.
The Berkeleys were a family
  Whose name from earliest age
Of Carolina's annals
  Appears on every page.
Before the war, their bondsmen
  By the hundreds could be told,
And the land was half a district [1]
  Which their head alone controlled.
At peace his slaves were freedmen,
  His lands were on his hands,
As the present of an elephant
  In Eastern story stands.
For them there was no market,
  Yet they were under tax,
Which simply confiscated,
  Yet would yearly greater wax.
Plantation on plantation
  Beneath the hammer fell,
Till the sheriff advertised at last
  He must the homestead sell.
"The Oaks" was what they styled it,
  A beautiful estate,[2]
In all the Southern country
  You would hardly find its mate.

And it, for generations,
  Had passed from head to son,
Among the Berkeley people,
  Ere their fortunes were undone.
They tried to chill the bidding,—
  For land was no demand,
And only speculators
  Were apt to be on hand:
A set of sharks who waited,
  On every day of sale,
During all of Reconstruction,
  Round the court house steps and jail,
In hopes to catch a bargain,
  And for a farthing buy
The home of widows, orphans,
  And turn them 'neath the sky.
And though I think it error
  When aught the law o'errules,
These men were sometimes beaten
  By their persecuted tools;
Or told (as by these Berkeleys,
  While the advertisement ran,)
"'Twas best on this occasion
  For them to have no plan;
'Twas meant to buy the property,
  At lowest price 'twould bring,
For Berkeley's wife — the owner
  Could thus to homestead cling."
So off they stood, like vultures
  Which circle round the sky,
While men stay near to corpses
  That still unburied lie.

But at the last a rumor
  Began to stir and grow,
That there would be a bidder,
  Whom Berkeley knew his foe.
He was the county senator,
  Had Bureau-Agent been,
And once, in course of duty,
  Knocked the Oaks to enter in.
They spurned him from the doorway,
  When they heard his hated name,
And told him the dogs should tear him,
  If ever again he came.
He was termed a carpet-bagger,
  For he came within the State
With one valise's contents,
  But intent t' accumulate.
And fortune in battalions,
  Not singly, sent her gifts,
As she's wont to do with blessings,
  Or ills, as humor shifts.
For Whitmire soon held office,
  Which once the Berkeleys filled,
While horses, rooms and equipage
  In thrift proclaimed him skilled.[3]
First Monday dawned; to traffic
  Crowds ever come that day,[4]
On foot, or horse, in buggy,—
  Drink sometimes makes affray,
The Berkeleys' friends and kindred,
  Well mounted men and brave,
Came early to the Court House,
  With talk and aspect grave;
With Whitmire came a rabble
  Of black militia there,
To which the band of Falstaff
  Would very well compare.
A fife and drum made discord,
  No step was ever kept,

At moves and rifle handling
  An Upton would have wept.[5]
These soldiers would, in conflict,
  Have scattered quick and blind,
But the Cavaliers were conscious
  Of the mighty North behind.
The auction was exciting,
  The Berkeley party bid
Their utmost means, but Whitmire
  Their very best outdid.
To raise a dollar strained them
  Than fifty once far worse,
And very low he gained it,
  'Mid many a muttered curse.
Then his troops, with mighty cheering,
  Paraded up and down,
A dozen times each highway
  And the public square in town.
Each sullen white was hooted,
  And while they marched in rank,
Large colored crowds beside them
  Ran on, with curious prank.
With apish tricks, preceded
  A clown, upon an ox,
While women halloaed "Glory!"
  And, dancing, flapped their frocks.
Each white aside stood darkly,
  And scarcely yielded way,
If on him in their marching
  The column chanced to stray.
Till sunset lingered Berkeley,
  With others used to rule,
And checked a dozen riots,
  And kept the young men cool.
He rode away at twilight,
  When half the crowd was gone,
And found the highways streaming
  As he to th' Oaks went on.

His wife and daughter waited,
  At their old residence,
All day to hear the tidings,
  In weeping and suspense.
They ate but little dinner;
  The dreary afternoon
Passed on the broad verandah
  Until uprose the moon.
Their supper was dispensed with
  Till Berkeley should arrive,
And finally to the gateway
  They went adown the drive.
Old Chloe followed with them,
  She had been the younger's nurse,
And had waited on the mother
  With a love unbought of purse.
They reached the gate, with pillars
  Surmounted high with balls,
And listened. Soon upon their ears
  A distant murmur falls.
It came from towards the Court House,
  And as it nearer drew,
They made it out militia
  Dispersing—drunken, too;
For they were yelling, hooting,
  And talking most obscene,
And firing, now a rifle,
  Then a pistol shot between.
The females closed the portal,
  Inside withdrew a space,
In hopes the rabble would pass on
  And not molest the place.
But they stopped afront the entrance,
  And loud, derisive talked
Of how their hero, Whitmire,
  Had Berkeley's bidding balked.
From this the trembling women
  Their adverse fortune learned;

But rising grief by terror
  Was quickly overturned.
On serenading Berkeley
  (Whose absence seemed unknown)
The crowd resolved, and entered
  The gateway, open thrown.
Of old who dared to visit
  Without a pass was scourged,
But now, ere fled the women,
  The mob around them surged.
It halted at their screaming,
  But quickly ribaldry,
And shouting and derision,
  Showed its hostility.
But suddenly a gallop
  Was heard adown the road,
And Berkeley burst upon them,—
  His face with anger glowed.
But if his rage was kindling,
  At their trespass, thus begun,
What felt he on discovering
  His dear ones near o'errun!
Forthwith there flashed his pistol,
  And cries of fear arose,
As with a random volley,
  Scattered his ebon foes.
Oblivious of their firing,
  He sprang from off his steed,
And to the cowering females
  Rushed headlong in his speed.
They saw his sudden entrance,
  His perilous attack
Upon a brutish multitude
  Who did not weapons lack.
A gun ball struck the mother,
  She sank in Chloe's arms,
And with one moan her soul hath flown
  Far from this earth's alarms.

Her daughter rushed to aid her,
　Saw the blood, and wildly fell
In fits of screaming, fainting,
　Which weeks could hardly quell.

The Oaks was splendid property,
　But ample for a duke,
So Whitmire seized occasion
　Th' old system to rebuke.
No land was owned by negroes,
　As yet, though eager sought,
Then whites to sell them thought it
　A shame, whate'er it brought.
(We learned full many a lesson,
　In Reconstruction days,
And now sell white or negro,
　Who can the money raise.)
So he cut half the property
　Into a hundred farms;
To purchase them the freemen
　Came flocking up in swarms
He sold them all they wanted,
　For credit or for cash,—
(Though those who took on credit
　Discovered they were rash.
He did not give them titles,
　But simply a receipt,
And promised them the papers
　When payments were complete.
Each moved upon his purchase,
　Paid more, improved it years,
But found when Whitmire sold the Oaks,—
　As afterwards appears,—
The gentleman who bought it
　Owned each undeeded home,
And, but for generosity,
　They must pay o'er or roam.)

These newly fledged freeholders,
　To build upon their land,
Buy all their former cabins,
　That in the quarters stand.
These quickly down are taken,
　And carted piecemeal on
Each buyer's farm though distant,
　And erected o'er anon.
Of quarters there were several;
　The largest one was seen
Some furlongs from the mansion,
　That crowned the whole demesne.
This quarter first was sold from;
　And only a single house
Was left a half year after,
　Your attention to arouse,
'Twas the overseer's dwelling,
　Around it was a field
Where in the earlier era
　The cabins were revealed.
Law gives the bankrupt homestead—
　Of very humble kind,
Compared to the great mansion
　That Berkeley left behind.
A thousand dollars only
　The sheriff laid aside,
From what the Oaks was sold for,
　This refuge to provide.
The court must make selection,
　And Whitmire interfered,
To mortify the enemy,
　Who at him once had sneered.
To place him in the cottage
　Where his overseer had dwelt,
While Whitmire moved to the mansion,
　Would be triumph keenly felt.
So this house, with fifty acres,
　As the homestead was approved

For Berkeley, by a circuit judge
   Whom Whitmire made and moved,
And vain protested Berkeley
   And counsel that he paid,
The court was firm, and ordered
   The investment to be made.
'Twas deep humiliation
   To take for future home
A place so near the mansion
   That he could see its dome.
Whither, of old, he'd lofty
   Wave off late traveler
That lodging asked, if aspect
   Might chance to give demur.
There were Berkeley, Allie, Chloe,
   (Still faithful) went along,
He farmed the field allotted,
   And brooded o'er each wrong;
He could not brook his fortune,
   And tried to drown his woe
By drinking deep, a remedy
   Oft tried by high and low.
And all the solemn lectures
   The world will ever hear
Will hardly make us temperate,
   When fortune serves severe.[6]
So the alien and negro make revel
   In the banqueting halls of the proud,
While the olden owner is toiling,
   And the mother is wrapped in the shroud.
And the daughter dreamily looketh,
   With her elbow at rest on the sill,
And her hand to her cheek, as she sitteth
   Each day at the house on the hill.
Ah Christ! when was there such a vision?
   That slender, tall, beautiful form,
The lustrous eye and the wavy hair,
   And the marble-cut, sinuous arm.[7]

Yes, wavy her hair, for 'tis loose to the air,
   And her dress is all crumpled and wild:
Ah, shame to the one who this fell work
     hath done,
   Who hath crazed this magnificent child!
Yes, crazed!—for months she lingered
   From the shock of her mother's death,
Her brain in whirl of fever,
   On fire her panting breath.
They long scarce hoped to save her,
   Yet at the last she rose,
But, alas! They found that madness
   Had seized her in its throes.
They tenderly waited on her,
   Her father, Chloe, too,
And sometimes one called Willie,
   Who had loved her, ere her rue.
She sits and mourns, but weeps not,
   Her gaze is forever kept on
Her olden home in the distance,
   Her thoughts on the days that are gone.
We think not how grateful is weeping,
   The reason may hang on a tear,
For it giveth a vent to the feelings
   Which, pent, into madness may flare.
Yet sometimes she'd roam to the churchyard,
   And you'd hear the deep moan
     and the sigh,
As she gazed on a wooden headmark,
   Though the tear glistened not in her eye.
That sculptureless grave contrasted
   With its neighbors, marble crowned;
For a century here her kindred
   Had made their burying ground;
But alone the murdered lady
   Of all lay under the soil,
Without a shaft to tell you
   She rested from her toil.

* * *

One day—a year from the auction—
  Young Allie was thus at the grave,
And sat till the dews of evening
  Began all things to lave,
Then, rising, her arms she foldeth,
  And fixedly stares at the Oaks,
Which looms above the tree-tops,
  Though the dusk her vision chokes.
At length she wildly starteth,
  And throweth her right hand up,
And she swears some oath as solemn,
  As if by the Holy Cup.
Then suddenly ceased her transport,
  She left the graveyard old,
And rapidly walked and stealthy
  Towards her home which had been sold.

Between the Oaks and Court House
  That night the meeting's held
Of the Loyal League, in forest
  And swamp unclaimed of eld.
A stump sufficed for altar,
  With stars and stripes 't was draped,
And laden with other emblems,
  In certain order shaped;
The Bible, Constitution,
  The Declaration, Sword,
The Ballot-box, and Sickle,
  And Gavel there were stored.
No Censer with Liberty's Fire
  Shone there,—as the ritual charged;
But a pine torch. Round this altar
  Their circle was formed, and enlarged
By numerous truants, who entered
  Past the sentinels posted around,
While the distant passer noticed
  A wild and wailing sound—

Peculiar to negro singing
  (Of which they justly brag,)
As they chanted "John Brown's Body,"
  Or "We'll Rally Round the Flag."
But each prayer and exhortation,
  Each oath and deep response,
Their gliding forms and shadows,—
  All these the woods ensconce.
They take in several members,
  With full and mystic rite,
Who are sworn to join the party
  Which burst their bonds in might.
Savage and weird the picture,—
  Salvator Rosa's brush
Had placed it on the canvas
  Such way your breath to hush.[8]
There first was trained the freedman
  In politics, debate;
And taught to love "the Party,"
  And his former masters hate.
There was instilled the lesson
  That it was right in turn
To steal from white oppressor,
  His residence to burn.
So nightly rose a flaming
  Far o'er the land to warn
That negro torch had kindled
  Some dwelling, gin or barn.
And with gun and baying watch-dog,
  You lightly slept of night,
And dreamed of fire and burglar,
  And wakened in affright.

But to-night their chairman's absent—
  'Twas Whitmire held the place—
They missed his thorough knowledge,
  And long familiar face.

1

They late dispersed. One cluster
 To approach the Oaks began,
All black, except a couple
 Of the carpet-bagging clan:
Some of the brood of vultures
 Who, when the battling ceased,
Thronged to the field and gorged till
 they reeled
 On their national garbage feast.
The negroes sang and holloaed,
 Or made peculiar cries
Which Southrons nightly list to
 As the negro homeward hies.
As they reached their homes they lingered,
 Till very few were left
When they passed by Berkeley's cottage,
 Where he dwelt of home bereft.
But then their uproar doubled,
 As they marched along the street,
They cursed his dogs for barking,
 And on his palings beat.
"The mad girl's not at her window,"
 One of the party said;
Another rejoined: "Let's raid them,
 Since for once we have caught her abed."
So when they had passed a little
 Two of the crowd returned,
And a chicken and turn of fence rails
 They bagged while they sojourned.
—Such were the persecutions
 Of Reconstruction time—
No wonder there were Ku Klux,
 No wonder there was crime!
I don't believe in bondage,
 Though Carolinian true,
And now regret that on us
 It ever cast its hue.

I hope in future era
 To see the negro rise
To worth of mind and character
 Which wins of life the prize.
But to turn him loose as master—
 A child in freedom's ways—
And make his owners subjects,
 Was this best way to raise?
God knows, perhaps 'twas better
 At once to meet the shock,
Extract the tooth, and bolt the dose,
 Not wear by drops the rock.
Wherever freedom dwelleth
 A certain course she'll take,
But sometimes charming fairy,
 And sometimes groveling snake.[9]
I'd fain have seen the negro
 Improve his chances great,
But he was simply human,
 And met the general fate.
For all the course of history
 Hath tended this to show:
That sudden revolutions
 Are apt to backward flow.
It takes well nigh a century,
 As proves each precedent,
One foot above the ocean
 To raise a continent.
The dropping of a delta
 Will take ten thousand years,
And countless ages to change rocks
 To fertile hemispheres.
So, too, with social order,
 With pleasures of mankind,
With all the thoughts and habits
 Like ivy round him twined,
They will not change of sudden,
 However hard you try,

But only after many
  Generations onward fly.
Clothe the mule with skin of lion,
  'Twill quickly come to pass
His braying will betray him,
  And show him still the ass.
The cat may change to lady,
  But when she sees a mouse,
She'll straightway leap upon him,
  And not scream o'er the house.
You may shave and paint the leopard,
  Whiten skin of Ethiop men,
But the spots and ebon color
  Will soon push out again.
The sow will to her wallow,
  To his vomit turn the dog;
And the devil's cloven foot appears,
  Howe'er he tries to clog.
And men may raze a Bastile,
  And use the guillotine
On many a proud aristocrat,
  And on the king and queen,
But empire quickly follows;
  Napoleon's worse than king;
And finally time's whirligig
  The Bourbons back will bring.
The early Christians gloried
  When their faith was made the state's;
But quickly found that baptism
  Changed no man's likes or hates.
The awful Roman city
  Named the universal church;
Of pagan rites and practices
  The converts went in search.
They were told to break their idols
  And bow to ideal God,
But 'tis ever human failing
  At abstract things to nod.

So very soon the images
  Of Virgin, Christ and saint
Were crowding Christian churches,
  Bowed to without restraint.[10]
And it proved artificial,
  Unnatural and wrong,
That blacks should rule the Saxon,
  Through Northern aid too long,—
Like angry ape, or Titmouse,
  With his thousands ten a year,[11]
While the law of mighty England
  Sustained him in his sphere.
The same blood welled in Southrons
  As those Bostonians had
Who threw the tea in ocean,
  With Indian guises clad;
And left alone, like spring bent,
  They rose with mighty power,
And the negro ceased fantastic tricks,
  And helpless 'gan to cower.

Well, our crowd went on commenting
  Where Whitmire was to-night,
"He promised to come, at tea-time,"
  Said one whose face was white;
"His family's in New England,
  We others, with one design,
Left his house to-night for the meeting,
  While he lingered to write a line."
Through fields of corn and cotton,
  And—such the times—broomsedge,
The thoroughfare ran ere touching
  The lawn's extended edge.
Then half a mile, the portal
  At last before them stood
Where the mob on Berkeley's lady
  Had wrought their work so good.

—I feel some disposition
  Just here to paint the place,
For it was truly lovely,
  And well deserves the space.
The people from a distance
  Who travel in the South,
When we boast of former splendor,
  Think we merely wish to mouth.
Our old ancestral homesteads
  Are ne'er from railway seen,
But only swamps and pinelands,
  Poor fields and buildings mean.
The old-time planters, fearing
  Near growth of noisy town,
And owning horse and equipage
  To ride to depots down,
Objected to surveyors
  Running upon them close,
So that a line of railroad
  E'er'd the poorest land engross.
But in each rural District
  Some two or three estates
Were ever found, whose splendor
  No pen exaggerates.
The balance of the County
  Might stunted be and poor,
And unto every gentleman
  Full many a slave and boor,
But that is simply stating
  We did the North precede:
Our planters to your Vanderbilts
  Had seemed in direst need!
I've strolled along Fifth Avenue,
  Where fifty millionaires dwell,
Whose wealth the other million
  New Yorkers' will excel.
And so with every country

That lies in human ken,
  In England half the realty
Belongs to a hundred men.
  A very few are happy,
    A very few are rich;
But most of poor humanity
  Is slaving in the ditch.
The strongest force in physics
  Is found to be evolved
When the greatest heap of matter
  Is consumed, and thus resolved.
So perhaps in mortal matters,
  The keenest happiness
Is witnessed where our neighbors
  Are put to most distress.
Oh! I have read and pondered
  On each book that Darwin wrote,
And over Herbert Spencer
  I once would fairly gloat,
And when on Nature gazing
  I own they speak the truth,
That the strongest are the fittest,
  And give the weakest ruth.
That through the boundless universe
  All beings have one aim—
Men, insects, beasts and flowers—
  To make each other game.
But though their observations
  Have made the churchmen quake,
And the orthodox conclusions
  As to Bible-science shake,
Though they've shown that nature's battling
  As we all admit who view,
Yet is this struggling moral?
  Does only good accrue?
I know that beast and savage
  Will extirpate the weak,
But is nature's state the model

For civilized men to seek?
If so, then Herbert Spencer
  Should have been impaled at once,
He was puny, and most people
  Believed him impious dunce.
Closed up should be each hospital,
  Each orphan house, free school,
Each means for dealing charity,
  Each move against misrule.
Yes, leave mankind to nature,
  Then Might alone is Right,
And those will take who have the power,
  Those keep who've strength to fight.[12]
But all of human history
  Has been a contest hard,
Of Right with Might, and Progress
  Trying Nature to discard.
And the foremost men and nations
  Have most of charity,
And, unlike the natural savage,
  Guard e'en beasts from tyranny.
And whether God or human,
  I know that Jesus Christ
Touched civilization's keynote,
  In language apt and spiced,
When he said "Do unto others
  As you'd have them do to you,"
And praised the good Samaritan
  Who saved the wounded Jew.
Let Spencer reason, using
  Every favorite thundering word,
(Which he's coining e'er, while censuring
  The classics as absurd,)
But the pupil of his Ethics
  May lay the book aside,
And kill or steal with conscience,
  If his crime he can but hide,
Like the people of old Sparta

Who did not deem it aught
  Of wrong to go a thieving,
  Unless the thief was caught.
Like Offitt the Bread Winner,
  Who felt a better man
When he had two men nigh murdered
  In his money getting plan.[13]

But this makes two digressions,
  A thing I quite abhor;
Pray spare:—'t is first I've published
  Unpruned by editor;
I've tried my wings and sported
  In most unwonted glee,
Because 't is strange sensation
  To feel at last I'm free.
Besides I do but copy
  The modern novel's style,
Which stops the tale to moralize
  So oft—'t is sometimes vile.
Yet of me've said some critics
  (Not knowing e'en my name,)
"To the gift of closely following
  His theme he has some claim."
Thanks; henceforth right I'll prove you,
  Or try; so let's retrace
Our steps, and join the strollers,
  Who had reached the Berkeley place.
The stately portal entered,
  They took the avenue,
Which pierced the lawn of oak trees
  And mat of Kentucky blue.
This passed, they reached the garden
  Of flowers, 'twixt house and lawn,
When whom do they meet in its pathways—
  Like a glorious dream of the dawn?
They stop, and glances mutual
  Exchange, all know her well;

But the maiden onward passes,
  And vanishes like a spell.
And they suddenly hear a crying,
  As of some one in despair,
Half smothered, in the mansion,
  Where there shines a brilliant glare!
A surmise—all go rushing
  Up steps, 'cross balcony,
Through hall, and down to cellar,
  Whence comes that awful cry.
The stair is barricaded,
  With barrels, wood, *debris*,
And the heap is freshly fired,
  But does not yet blaze free.
They do not stop or linger,
  But rush to the attack,
The flames are soon extinguished,
  But leave their mark of black.
Then the cellar quick is opened,
  And gasping in his fright
They find their leader 'prisoned,
  Who had missed the tryst to-night!
Ah, he will ne'er forget it!
  His agony, despair!
When the maiden burst upon him,
  And signalled to the stair;
And followed,—tea just over—
  —Her pistol cocked in hand—
Till she turned the key upon him,
  No help at his command.
The cellar in old era
  Had held its store of wine;
But under its new owner
  Had a very changed design.
He was militia-Colonel,
  And for their armory
His cellar had been chosen,
  As if by destiny.

And in it then was quartered
  A store of uniforms,
Of rifles, bayonets, powder,
  And cartridges in swarms.
And if that fire had lasted,
  And burnt the Oaks to ground,
The explosion, like an earthquake,
  Would have shaken the counties round.
She had seen by the straggling troopers
  Her mother's life o'erthrown;
She knew their evil leader
  Had made the Oaks his own.
She had heard the talk (in silence)
  Of father and his friends,
When the new possessor altered
  The old wine cellar's ends,
And she had watched the wagons,
  Which, with militia throng,
And heaped with their equipments,
  Passed to the Oaks along.
And she pointed to them, saying,
  As she marched him in to-night:
"Your weapons killed my mother
  But their owner now shall smite!"
She caged him with no exit,
  And built a barricade
As for funeral pile, he trembled,
  And vainly mercy prayed;
No word she ever uttered,
  But when her task was done
She sat outside, in vigil,
  Till half the night was run.
Then she struck a match, he heard it,
  He screamed to her, to God,
Till he lost his breath, and his heart beat
  In his breast like a thrasher's rod.

\* \* \*

134

Of course there was sensation,
  Both very deep and wide,
When Allie's act was published,
  As usual magnified.
The Stalwart press devoted
  Some columns each per day,
To showing how rebellion
  Again was in array.
And a motion passed the Senate
  (See the Journal of that date),[14]
At once t' appoint Committee
  To go, and investigate;
With power to send for persons,
  And papers, and to sit
In any distant city,
  If the Oaks would not permit.
To the Probate Judge went Whitmire,
  Intent to crush his foe,
And to the State Asylum
  He swore that she should go.
The papers *de lunatico*
  Are very quickly filed;
A day's set for the hearing,—
  Her father's grief is wild.
And wild, too, is her lover,
  Young Willie, who has clung
Through all to her since childhood;
  And Chloe, too, is stung.
They importune their foeman,
  He swears to have no check;
All the State and Union army
  Are at his call and beck.
And ere the time appointed
  Full many a sleepless night
These faithful three pass weeping
  And praying in their plight.
But every thing is hopeless,
  The prison seemed her lot,

And there was naught could save her
  From the deep and thickening plot!

*Your captors e'en now are assembling,*
  *To tear thee from all that was thine,*
*And I feel that your fingers are trembling,*
  *As I madly encase them in mine.*
*Ah! This of all yet is the hardest,*
  *And evils past number have thronged;*
*To part us, to take thee, my darling,*
  *Indeed, 't is the worst they have wronged.*

*You would linger all day by the curtain;*
  *To strangers you seldom gave heed;*
*Yet one step to rouse you was certain,*
  *And you heard it when service e'er freed.*
*For you blushed and were silent*
    *with worship,*
  *As I drew up my chair to your side,*
*And toyed with your ringlets,*
*caressed you,*
  *And called you my Allie, my bride.*

*But all my fond visions are blighted,*
  *That reason will never return;*
*They bear you from those who delighted*
  *To tend you, to those who will spurn.*
*Yet nay! I know well that e'en strangers*
  *Will start when they gaze on your face,*
*And wait on you constant and tender;*
  *But the home-life they cannot replace.*

*And can it be that you will miss me,*
  *As you pine in your cheerless brick cell?*
*If we e'er meet again will you kiss me,*
  *And know him who loved you so well?*
*Yes! Absence ne'er conquers true passion;*
  *My heart will go with you afar,*

*And yours will stay with me, my darling,*
  *Though they part us by distance and bar.*

*And we will meet! ill lasts not forever!*
  *A just God's in heaven above;*
*And I feel that He'll suffer it never,*
  *Such hate e'er to smother His love.*
*The spoiler shall yet meet*
    *with vengeance,*
  *The bondsman he chastened for pride;*
*And your reason shall come with the*
    *tide-turn,*
  *And then I shall call you my bride!*

*Ah! shame to you, shame to you!*
  *Who would have believed*
*You'd e'er be so cruel*
  *To those you'd aggrieved?*
*You slaughtered their kinsmen,*
  *You conquered their band,*
*You turned free their bondsmen,*
  *And stole all their land.*

*You drove them from homestead,*
  *The mother you crushed,*
*The daughter you maddened,*
  *At nothing you blushed.*
*And now when the maiden*
  *Does what she knows not,*
*She's dragged from her loved ones*
  *—The prison her lot.*

*Ah, this is not justice!*
  *—My brothers just freed,*
*Will you back up the alien,*
  *E'en in his worst deed?*
*Oh, no ! as God liveth*
  *You should not do this;*

*Ah! have you forgotten*
  *Your kindly old Miss?*

*She came to the cabins*
  *To visit the sick,*
*The girls for weddings*
  *She ever would trick.*
*If a slave, in her presence,*
  *Was doomed to the lash,*
*She'd beg for and save him,*
  *With cheek like the ash.*

*But ah! the good lady,*
  *Is laid in the grave!*
*The soft heart was broken,*
  *That pitied the slave!*
*And now her poor daughter,*
  *Of reason bereft,*
*Is all that old Chloe*
  *Can claim to have left.*

*For I nursed her dear mother,*
  *And then I nursed her;*
*And I'll cling to the poor child,*
  *Though all men deter!*
*Alas! She now needs me*
  *Far more than at first;*
*And if you should part us,*
  *Your deed is accurst.*

Well, over is the trial,
  Where mighty crowd was seen,
Of course there was no contest,
  No plea to intervene.
Her friends ask simply mercy,
  But sternly are refused,
Though promising her freedom
  Shall be ne'er again abused.

The mad-house is her sentence,
 The judge adjourns the court,
A deadly silence follows,—
 Man ask if this be sport?
Then such a storm arises
 As seldom gathers head,
For hundreds swore they'd guard her
 Until their blood ran red.
They snatched her ere the sheriff
 Took charge, and marched away,
A colored posse followed
 With very short delay;
Then the wildest scene of riot
 Was witnessed in the town,
But when Saxon meets the negro,
 The negro's quickly down.
In less than thirty minutes,
 No colored man was seen,
Save two or three who lingered,
 Stretched out upon the green.
And what became of Whitmire
 No man exactly knew,
He disappeared like magic,—
 To far off city flew.

That night a mystic column
 Filed o'er the chiefest road,
On horses clothed with housings,
 That to their ankles flowed.
Each rider too was hooded,
 Each wore a gown and mask,
And each was strapped with weapons,
 Ready for deadly task.
They steadfast onward traveled,
 The negro quaked and feared,
Who saw that ghastly cavalcade,
 As from his hut he peered.

But no one they molested,
 That night; they traveled on
Till the first faint streaks of morning
 Showed gloom was nearly gone.
Then the mystic column faded,
 With night, as sun uprose,
And the news spread through the county
 They had saved her from her foes.
To distant State they bore her,
 For years none knew the place,
Because all through the country
 Dwelt Berkeley's kin and race.
And she was gently cared for
 Away from olden scenes,
And Whitmire never found her,
 Though he freely lavished means.
Her father at his cottage
 Dwelt on in quiet gloom,
While Chloe went with Allie,
 To share her every doom.
I don't approve of Ku Klux,
 Nor Nihilistic plan,
My blood is mainly English,—
 Likes the fairly fighting man.
But I have seen oppression
 So cruel, absolute,
I glow to hear of vengeance,
 Though philosophy dispute.
And Allie, years thereafter,
 When mind again was clear,
Would ever detest the cruel,
 And the ones who domineer;
She was not consistent always,
 —(Perhaps her reason still,
On the subject of a tyrant
 Will always serve her ill.)
And though it seems strange fountain
 From which to hear such creed,—

A Southern planter's daughter,
  Not of the Commune breed,—
Yet I have heard her urging
  That when oppressors smite,
It is right to make resistance,
  "E'en," she'll sing, "with dynamite!

"Oh! take the awful tyrant
  Whom the Russians call the Czar,
With his knout, police and army
  And Siberian mines afar;[15]
And take the wailing people,
  Ever cowering in affright,—
And can you blame them turning
  In despair to dynamite?

"Ah! all the world was startled,
  When it heard his father's fate;
But a wife he had discarded,
  For a mistress kept in state;
And to squander on her millions
  Taxed a thousand homes to blight—
Oh think of this, and wonder
  Why they threw the dynamite!

"What does the Czar with jewels,
  When myriads are in need?
Why rules he sixty million
  Purer men, of kindred breed?
Will he let them meet and organize
  To give him equal fight?
—Oh, no! he strikes unfairly,
  So they take to dynamite.

"Think on the Irish landlord—
  Whose fathers robbed the land
From the father of his tenants,
  Whose rights on bayonets stand.

A thousand squalid renters
  Their little means unite
To buy him London's fatness,—
  Till they rush to dynamite.

"O despots, tremble everywhere,
  Your doom is knelling now!
For men have cool and stern resolved
  No more to you to bow.
We will obey no ruler,
  Save to choose we have the right;
And if he tries to hand of mail,
  We'll fight with dynamite!

"We hail the name of Brutus!
  We hail the name of Tell!
And own with bow and dagger
  They served their tyrants well;
But a Gessler now, or Caesar,
  Will feel redoubled fright,
For the future Tell and Brutus
  Will be armed with dynamite![16]

"In many a million hovel,
  Or ghastly tenement,
Are a billion creatures starving,—
  Though their lives are slaving spent.
Yet a Gould to cut their wages
  E'er is watching like a kite,
And the public's damned by Vanderbilt,
  —Despite their dynamite.

"Oh! Jesus tells the story
  Of the good Samaritan,
Who, while the others passed aside,
  Gave help to dying man.
So while around our firesides,
  Where wealth and cheer delight,

Let's spare for human suffering,
  —It may banish dynamite."

Our story takes a recess
  Of six or seven years,
Ere Allie on the stage again
  And at the Oaks appears.
To Whitmire come promotions
  So great, that rural scenes
He quits, and seeks Columbia,
  Where harvests fat he gleans.
A mansard roof receives him,
  A fountain plays in front,
To sport with steed and landaulet
  Is constantly his wont.
He sold the Oaks on moving,
  And Willie's father bought,
The acres half were lessened,
  But the house unchanged in aught.
'Twas opened warm to Berkeley,
  Who both was far too proud
To take of alms, and t' enter
  The Oaks no more had vowed.
Will's father had been lucky,
  Some fortune he had saved,
And son, and father also,
  Had well their troubles braved.
They went to work right nobly
  Like many Southrons, then,
And proved not mere patricians,
  But self supporting men.
(Oh, Northern people, watch it!
  The coming Southern race,
In arts and money-making,
  Are going to give you chase!
'Twas sternest of necessity
  That forced them to the plow,

But of himself each Southerner
  Can take the best care now.
Some of the olden manners
  Could not sustain the fight,
And, moping, brooding, drinking,
  Soon sank from public sight.
But now no work's degrading,—
  Too many of the ton
Are plowing, clerking, teaching,—
  All sneer at idle Don.
I now think slavery error;
  Although the North must own
'Tis hardly found entitled
  First at us to've thrown the stone.
You, too, had slaves once; tenements
  Our negro quarters beat,
The master kept the aged—
  Where's your laborer's retreat?
And, as usual with an evil,
  It had its side of good,—
Half civilized the Afric
  Brought to our neighborhood.
But the old Plantation era
  Is passed fore'er away,
And I rejoice that slavery
  Has seen its final day.
I see the State improving
  In numbers now and wealth,
So wondrously, I own it:
  "Our old life was not health!"
Our land is filled with engines,
  With factories and mines;
And Progess, the iconoclast,
  Is breaking olden shrines,
There's no one now can tarry,
  No time is there for play,
For Satan takes the hindmost,
  And the smartest wins the day.)

\* \* \*

'Twas—76, and Hampton
  His famous circuit rode,
And all the State with tumult
  From hills to sea o'erflowed.
And when the hot election
  Results in contest, doubt,
And Union bayonets grimly
  Keep Hampton's party out;
But all the signs are pointing
  To his success at last,—
Then Berkeley brings back Allie,
  Regardless of the past.
And Chloe, old and feeble,
  With her returns at length;
Still madness clings to Allie,
  Though scarce with former strength.
She had been melancholy
  And silent when away,
But remembered Berkeley's cottage,
  As if not gone a day.
She showed some little gladness,
  Then took her window seat,
And at the Oaks intently
  She gazed with olden heat.
She warmly greeted Willie,
  Her father, too, she knew,
But of her ancient neighbors
  Remembered very few.
A week or two passed over,
  Then words and posture showed
A strange hallucination
  Within her forehead glowed.
She seemed like one expectant,
  And ever waiting now,
And not with brooding sadness
  As formerly to bow.

While now and then she'd murmur,
  As if in self amaze,
"I thought I would have heard it
  Long since, or seen the blaze."
And if she chanced to notice
  One moving toward the Oaks,
To him she beckons warnings
  And not to go invokes.
She evidently fancied
  Her prisoner still secure,
And the debris still burning,
  The loud explosion sure!
The doctors gave opinion,
  A crisis was at hand,
When mania would forsake her,
  Or turn to stronger brand.
Quite urgent were their cautions
  To guard from every chance
Of sudden, strong excitement,
  Which might th' event advance.

The papers meanwhile daily
  Were filling every page
With burnings, stealings, shootings,
  Such was the races' rage.
And all throughout the county,
  Both main and private road,
Each night with red-clad horsemen,
  Patrolling, overflowed;[17]
And e'en the court house village
  Was guarded, too, till day,
Yet many a conflagration
  Still shone with reddening ray.
One night while dragged the contest
  Her love spent the eve
With Allie till his column
  Should pass, when he must leave.

Quite mournful his reflections,
  As he sat her hand in grasp;
"Oh! is there naught can save her,
  And snatch from madness' grasp?
So young as yet, so lovely,
  She stirs like music's self;
To cure her I would squander,
  If mine, the wide world's pelf.
She wakes in me emotions
  No other's sight can rouse,
My breast will e'er be vacant
  If heaven our parting allows,
For my heart has been torn from my bosom,
  And placed on her tender shrine.
God grant that her reason, like sunshine,
  May break forth—and then she'll be mine."
But his comrades call, he leaveth,
  While, with the weird look of a seer,
She says, "Good-night, 't is coming,
  Revenge at last is near."


The column on their mission
  Adown the road deploy,
And watch till all aweary
  Their relief is hailed with joy.
As they repass the cottage,
  They see by the light within
That Allie is still at the window,
  And she starts at their passing din,
And open throws the sashes,
  And utters loud the cry:
"Approach not! it is coming!
  Revenge's sweet hour is nigh!"
Then she points to the old mansion,
  Where all the horsemen stare,
And they start and cry of sudden,
  For there shines a brilliant glare!

A streak of fire is stealing
  And creeping up the house,
They gallop wildly to it,
  And the sleeping inmates rouse.
The Oaks burns fast, —no buckets—
  The reservoir on top
Has long been idle ornament,
  About to pieces drop.
The match of negro prowlers
  Had done its fatal work;—
They haunted bush and thicket
  Would in your outgrounds lurk;
They'd dodge the patrol; watch-dogs
  They'd hush with poisoned meat,
Then break, steal, fire, or outrage,
  With Indian's noiseless feet.—
From all attempts to extinguish
  They very soon withdrew,
And fell to moving furniture,
  'Twas all that they could do.
Among the things they rescued
  Was the famous cellar's store;
You'll feel surprised, as armory
  To hear 't was used once more.
The Rifle Club would gather
  At the Oaks as central place;
Of weapons, powder, cartridges
  Was stored there many a case.


From wood-heap in piazza
  The fire sprang, 't was found;
It traversed side and roofing,
  Ere inside or to ground.
So all the cellar's contents,
  And those of parlor, room,
They save before the dwelling
  Is half of flames a tomb.

Then sadly from the garden
   They look upon the blaze,
When sudden a mournful object
   Attracts their wondering gaze.
'Twas the maddened maiden dancing,
   Not far adown the lawn,—
Spread to breeze her tresses—
   As lovely as a fawn.
And presently notes of music,
   As sweet as a dying bird's,
Trilled from her lips of ruby,—
   Though wild the stirring words:

*"O tramp not on the serpent,*
   *Or his venomous tooth will strike;*
*And kick not the sickened lion,*
   *For strength may revive with dislike.*
*Throw down what you spurn with a caution,*
   *For often there cometh recoil;*
*Be careful to stand from the building,*
   *Your hands would tear down and despoil.*

*"You have trampled on the serpent,*
   *And the weakened lion struck,*
*You have thrown us to earth with our*
     *fortunes,*
   *—You have sipped the sweet chalice*
     *of luck!*
*But a bell in the distance is ringing,*
   *And there flaps at your window a wing,*
*The dead form of vengeance is crouching,*
   *And nothing will save from his spring!"*

Her lover tried to calm her,
   But wilder fast she grew,
And when the flames high-mounted,
   Out from the lawn she flew;
She beckoned all to follow,

And cried: "'Tis here at last,
Flee far from the fated mansion,
   In time to escape from the blast."
To all it was apparent
   She thought her olden foe
Was still within the cellar,
   Where she fastened him long ago;
And she was madly certain
   The house with mighty noise
Would soon blow up, and kill him,
   So at the gate she joys.
Then sudden, like the lightning,
   Flashed a thought on Willie's brain,
And he hastens to call the gazers,
   And his lucky device explain.
He had heard, he said, that one's reason
   Is often awakened, when lost,
By the sudden seeing or meeting with things
   Which your path in old time had crossed.
And if sudden and strong emotion
   From its place first shook the mind,
If reshaken by passion severe as the first,
   'Twill again to its place be consigned.
So he seized a keg of powder,
   And wrapped it thick around
With several blankets, wetted,
   Which lying round he found.
No words will stop, he warns them
   To leave the dangerous place;
They go, and he waiteth patient,
   Till he sees them off some space.
Then shouldering keg, he chargeth,
   Mounts flaming porch, and throws
His burden far in the hall way
   Where yet no fire glows.
Then off he springs and races,
   As never he raced before,
Half-charred with lapping flame-tongues,

And deafened by their roar.
He rushes down the avenue,
  But stops when half the way,
And behind an ancient oak tree
  He crouches,—and well he may;
There comes a sound terrific,
  And volcanic, meteor flash,
And the grand old Berkeley mansion
  Hath met its final crash.
The fragments, like vast rockets,
  Rise to heaven and fall again,
And the fearful boom and its echoes
  Shake the country, and rouse all men.
And then the gleam of madness
  Shone fierce in the maiden's eye,
And she wildly danced by the flaming
  That reddened the midnight sky:

*"Oh do not press the Russian,*
  *Or he burns his proudest town!*
*O do not goad a Samson,*
  *Or he teareth the temple down!*

*"You have goaded the blinded Samson,*
  *And the fleeing Russian pressed,*
*And song and legend forever*
  *Their vengeance will attest."*

They lead her away to the cottage,
  She laughs and sings as she goes;
Her mania, alas! seems strengthened,
  And all through the night it grows.
She does not rise in the morning,
  A crimson fever burns;
She lies long weeks, and raveth,
  But at last the illness turns;
And she lies there quiet and feeble,
  And pale, her sweet eyes closed;

Long time she lay there silent,
  But she wakened at length composed!
Round the strange room looked she wondering,
  And then for her mother called,—
Ah, bitter at first the waking,
  But madness was disenthralled!
Her Willie was her savior,
  By his perilous wild design,
And his splendid hero's promptness,
  When there was no time to refine.
The delusion all absorbing
  That held her brain in throe
Was by th' explosion gratified,—
  And then it had to go:

This almost ends my story;—
  About a year was passed
Ere Will and Allie wedded,
  But it came about at last.
It happened at the capital
  Where both their fathers dwell,
And hold again high office
  Since black dominion fell.
Old Chloe waited on her,
  And tottered in delight,
"She had decked old Miss at her wedding,
  And why not Miss Allie to-night?"
As Willie's marriage present,
  His father gave the Oaks,
Insurers had rebuilt it
  Ere had cleared away its smokes.
And Allie in the church yard—
  Sought ought the earliest day—
Cried much (not all in sorrow),
  Upon her first survey.
A tall but broken column
  Of frosted marble is there,

And carved her mother's name and this:
  "How long, O Lord?" appear.
And in a gloomy dungeon,
  Within the prison of State,
A familiar form was lying,
  While the wedding guests were elate.
It was the carpet-bagger
  Whom Allie would once have slain,
At last to justice accounting
  For the larcenous crimes of his reign,
But very joyful Whitmire
  When his eyes with the sun were unclosed,
For they brought him the Governor's pardon,
  —But terms were there imposed:
"You're pardoned, her prayer hath saved you,
  But this I must ordain,
That you go from the State where you glutted
    your hate,
  And never come back again."
And working on a railway,
  In after years, a gang
Were seen of dusky convicts,
  'Twas better far to hang!
(Alas! if ever torture
  That passeth human speech,
Grinds soul and mind to brutishness,
  And frame past cure of leech,
Was ever seen 'mong prisoners,—
  E'en on the galley bench—
'Tis where the leasing system
  Emits its putrid stench.
Ah! blot it out forever!
  —Take not my single word,
But let the voice of Cable
  And all the world be heard![18]
But I've seen to censure prisons
  All through this mighty land,—

State, county, Northern, Southern,
  In shameful plight they stand;
They're freezing in the winter,
  In summer are Black Holes,
With vermin, filth, poor feeding,—
  While jailor-brute controls.
More service get the clients
  Whom I see in jail confined,
Than those on bail,—my pity
  Rouses all my soul and mind.
We justly may imprison,
  But not torture at the stake.
O shade of Howard warm us,
  O politicians wake!
Grand-juries, ever shallow,
  Presentments cease to file
Praising the jail's good order!
  —Report the system vile!)[19]
Among them those whose torches
  Had fired the mansion last,
That night when Allie, dancing,
  At last heard the terrible blast;
These too were given freedom,
  Will's plea their pardon won,—
He owned that by their arson
  Was Allie's cure begun.
And after a due conviction,
  And a year or two of pain,
Knowing their evil counsels,
  He saved them from the bane,
Then, too, it pleased his Allie,
  Who, sane, is ever crossed
With pain, if any enemy
  In revenge is put to cost.
She is ever kind and tender
  To every thing that's frail,
Will weep if hound is bleeding,[20]
  And e'er start at human wail.

And sometimes she composes
　A verse or plaintive song,
Which always counsels pity
　When the weak offend the strong.

*Oh stop! Think as above me*
　*You stand to strike the blow,*
*That I've had few to love me,*
　*And much to undergo.*
*For fortune never brightly*
　*Shone on my pathway lone,*
*No food by day, and nightly*
　*My head upon the stone!*
*And it was far more mournful*
　*Beneath the load to bend,*
*Because the world was scornful,*
　*And quick to reprehend.*
*O then, how can you wonder*
　*That I should bitter be,*

*That I should slay and plunder*
　*To 'scape from misery?*
*I will not say 'tis rightful*
　*To stain your hands with crime,*
*But poverty is frightful,*
　*Endurance is sublime!*
*And think if I have deeply*
　*My hands in sin imbued,*
*The world might once so cheaply*
　*Have saved what has ensued.*
*You'd own if you had sadly*
　*Been forced my life to live,*
*You must have done as badly;*
　*Then can you not forgive?*
*O I would mind it scarcely*
　*With even death to meet,*
*Since fate has served so fiercely,*
　*Yet spare me—life is sweet.*

\* \* \*

145

# Notes

## INTRODUCTION

[1] [Belton O'Neall Townsend,] "South Carolina Morals," *Atlantic Monthly* 39, no. 234 (April 1877).

[2] Telephone conversation, Eugene N. Zeigler Jr. with the editor.

[3] "Interesting Life Story Belton O'Neal [sic] Townsend A Founder This County," *Florence Morning News*, February 5, 1939, insert p. 2; phone call Eugene N. Zeigler Jr. with the editor.

[4] George McD. Stoll, "Biographical Introduction," copy at South Caroliniana Library, University of South Carolina (hereafter Caroliniana). This four-page promotional brochure, published separately, ostensibly was the work of Stoll, a fifty-two year-old real-estate broker. However, Townsend's grandson Nick Zeigler suspected it actually was written by Townsend. Telephone conversation, Eugene N. Zeigler Jr. with the editor.

[5] Biograpical information on Belton O'Neall Townsend (hereafter BOT) has been supplied by Stoll, "Biographical Introduction"; "Interesting Life Story"; Eugene N. Zeigler Jr. to the editor, telephone conversations and December 10, 1996 letter; G. Wayne King, *Rise Up So Early: A History of Florence County, South Carolina* (Spartanburg: Reprint Co., 1981), 95-98; and census records.

[6] On Townsend's academic record, see Stoll, "Biographical Introduction," and commencement summaries in *The Daily Phoenix* (Columbia, S.C.), June 30, 1871, June 30, 1872, June 29, 1873.

[7] When the General Assembly chose Chamberlain to be a South Carolina College trustee in February 1873, he received fifty votes out of eighty-seven cast in the South Carolina house and fifteen out of twenty in the senate. By contrast, ex-Governor Robert K. Scott received a single vote in each chamber. *The Daily Phoenix* (Columbia, S.C.), February 15, June 29, 1873.

[8] Belton O'Neall Townsend Papers, Caroliniana.

[9] Transcription of BOT to Mary Brow Townsend, November 4, 1870, Belton O'Neill Townsend Family History Folder, Darlington County Historical Commission, Darlington, S.C. (hereafter Darlington Co. Historical Comm.) and in the Special Collection, James A. Rogers Library, Francis Marion University, Florence, S.C. (hereafter FMU).

[10] Ibid.

[11] Euphradian Society minutes, 1859-1873, Reel 2, Volume 9, 335-444,

University Archives, Caroliniana.

[12] Ibid., 345, 348, 355, 364.

[13] Ibid., 372, 381, 384, 399.

[14] Ibid., 411.

[15] [Townsend,] "South Carolina Morals."

[16] Euphradian Society minutes, 1859-1873, Reel 2, Volume 9, 412.

[17] Belton O'Neall Townsend Family History Folder, Darlington Co. Historical Comm., and Special Collections, FMU.

[18] "Interesting Life Story"; Eugene N. Zeigler Jr. to the editor, telephone conversation. On J. Knox Livingston, see *Cyclopedia of Eminent and Respectable Men of the Nineteenth Century* (1892; Spartanburg, S.C.: The Reprint Co., 1973), I: 186-88; Emily Bellinger Reynolds and Joan Reynolds Faunt, *Biographical Director of the Senate of the State of South Carolina, 1776-1964* (Columbia: South Carolina Department of Archives and History, 1964), I: 941-42.

[19] William Dean Howells (hereafter WDH) to BOT, December 19, 1874, transcript in Belton O. Townsend: Misc., Townsend Papers, Darlington Co. Historical Comm. and FMU.

[20] WDH to BOT , June 14, 1876, ibid.

[21] WDH to Mary Brow Townsend, July 11, 1876, ibid. Although the circumstances are unclear, it is quite possible Mrs. Townsend, alarmed when Howells seemed about to publish her son's work, sent the photo, together with a request for anonymity because of the turmoil of Reconstruction politics.

[22] WDH to BOT, October 11, 1876, ibid.

[23] Ibid., October 16, 1876.

[24] [Belton O'Neall Townsend,] "A Southern Camp," *New York Tribune*, October 14, 1876. Walter Allen reproduced much of the first letter in *Governor Chamberlain's Administration in South Carolina: A Chapter of Reconstruction in the Southern States* (New York: G. P. Putnam's Sons, 1888), 398-402, and asserts its author subsequently succumbed to the "tyrannous electioneering" about which he wrote. How Allen knew this actually happened is unclear. The next four paragraphs are all taken from this first *Tribune* article.

[25] [Belton O'Neall Townsend,] "A Southern Camp," *New York Tribune*, October 16, 1876.

[26] Charleston *News and Courier* (hereafter *N&C*), October 17, 1876. On October 21, 1876, the *Tribune* printed dissenting opinion from readers living in Fort Motte, Eastover, and Chester, S.C.

²⁷ *N&C*, October 17, 1876. Dawson had written in the *News and Courier* on May 9 that it would be "folly" to run a candidate against Chamberlain, at the same time endorsing Democrats for other offices: "With Mr. Chamberlain as Governor, and a Conservative Democratic majority, or thereabouts in the lower house, the State, in every sense of the word, would be safe. In attempting to gain more, we might lose everything."

²⁸ *New York Times*, December 16, 1876.

²⁹ [Belton O'Neall Townsend,] "The Political Condition of South Carolina," *Atlantic Monthly* 39, no. 232 (February 1877).

³⁰ [Belton O'Neall Townsend,] "South Carolina Morals."

³¹ [Belton O'Neall Townsend,] "South Carolina Society," *Atlantic Monthly* 39, no. 236 (June 1877).

³² *N&C*, February 7, 1876. Italics in original. Ironically, Townsend regularly praised Dawson for his strong stands against the white Hamburg rioters. Townsend's repetition of detailed financial figures—property values, taxation, bond valuations—mirrors Dawson's style, and he no doubt gained much of his ammunition from the pages of the *News and Courier*.

³³ Frederick Jackson Garrison to WDH, March 22, 1877, and WDH to Frederick Jackson Garrison, April 25, 1877, transcripts in Belton O. Townsend: Misc., Townsend Papers, Darlington Co. Historical Comm. and FMU.

³⁴ WDH to BOT, August 28, 1877, transcripts in Belton O. Townsend: Misc., Townsend Papers, Darlington Co. Historical Comm. and FMU.

³⁵ Ibid.

³⁶ WDH to BOT, September 26, 1877, ibid.; [Belton O'Neall Townsend,] "The Result in South Carolina," *Atlantic Monthly* 41, no. 243 (January 1878).

³⁷ Transcript in Belton O. Townsend: Misc., Townsend Papers, Biographical Folder, Darlington Co. Historical Comm. and FMU.

³⁸ Andrew Hilen, ed., *The Letters of Henry Wadsworth Longfellow* (6 vols.; Cambridge: Harvard University Press, 1966-82), VI: 365-66.

³⁹ "Interesting Life Story"; Belton O. Townsend: Misc., Townsend Papers, Biographical Folder, Darlington Co. Historical Comm. and FMU; and *N&C*, August 1, 1882.

⁴⁰ *Florence Times*, March 14, 1883; "Biographical Introduction"; Belton O. Townsend: Misc., Townsend Papers, Biographical Folder, Darlington Co. Historical Comm. and FMU. On W. H. Day, see *Cyclopedia of Eminent and Respectable Men*, I: 484-85.

⁴¹ "Lawyer Campaigned on New County Issue," *Florence Morning News*,

October 4, 1970, 4E.

[42] *Pee Dee Index*, April 17, 1883.

[43] Grandson Nick Zeigler owned the copy sent to Gladstone; those given to Butler, the Euphradian Society, and several friends are at the Caroliniana.

[44] "Biographical Introduction."

[45] *N&C*, May 26, 31, 1884.

[46] *Columbia Register*, May 29, 1884, *Carolina Spartan*, June 4, 1884, and *The Nation*, June 26, 1884.

[47] WDH to BOT, May 14, 1884, transcript in Belton O. Townsend: Misc., Townsend Papers, Darlington Co. Historical Comm. and FMU. This letter indicates that Cary Townsend lived in Boston for a time and had some association with Howells. It is unclear whether Belton and Howells ever met. A review that appeared in the *Atlantic Monthly*, July 1884, probably written by Howells, echoed the sentiments expressed in this letter: "Mr. Townsend surely need not have published these verses. They show so much general talent of another sort than poetical that among his qualities should have been some reverence for poetry as art. He has treated poetry as if it were a mere accident."

[48] Frederick Anderson, William M. Gibson, and Henry Nash Smith, eds., *Selected Mark Twain-Howells Letters, 1872-1910* (Cambridge, Mass.: Belknap Press, 1967), 229. Aldrich succeeded Howells as editor of the *Atlantic Monthly* in 1881. Although Twain liked Aldrich, he had no illusions concerning the quality of his work and disliked Mrs. Aldrich intensely. Early in their relationship, Aldrich, without informing his wife, brought Twain home to dinner. Mrs. Aldrich, distressed by Twain's western demeanor and somewhat inebriated state, delayed eating until after he departed. Ron Powers, *Mark Twain: A Life* (New York: Free Press, 2003), 308-09.

[49] Anderson, *Selected Mark Twain-Howells Letters*, 230.

[50] WDH to BOT, August 30, 1884, transcript in Belton O. Townsend: Misc.,Townsend Papers, Biographical Folder, Darlington Co. Historical Comm. and FMU.

[51] "Criticism on Plantation Lay and Other Poems" (n.p., copy in the Caroliniana).

[52] Ibid.

[53] *N&C*, January 8, 1889.

[54] W. D. Howells, *The Minister's Charge; Or, The Apprenticeship of Lemuel Barker*, intro. by Howard M. Munford (Bloomington: Indiana University Press, 1978), xi-xvi.

[55] Darlington Co. Historical Comm. and FMU.

[56] Eugene N. Zeigler Jr. to the editor, December 10, 1996; telephone conversation, Eugene N. Zeigler Jr. with the editor.

[57] Norment Family History Folder, Darlington Co. Historical Comm.

[58] Belton O'Neall Townsend Family History Folder, Darlington Co. Historical Comm. and FMU.

[59] *Pee Dee Index*, June 9, 1886.

[60] Eugene Noel Zeigler Sr., thirteenth in a family of fourteen children, was born on Christmas Day 1887 and thus received the middle name of "Noel." His wife tried without success to get people to call their son, Eugene Noel Zeigler Jr., by that same name. Instead, the boy's step-grandfather, Daniel Malloy McEachin, once remarked that the youngster was a bad little boy, a "Young Nick" with the "Old Nick" in him, and it stuck. Eugene N. Zeigler Jr. to the editor, December 10, 1996. Leah Townsend's writings include "South Carolina Baptists, 1670-1800," (PhD dissertation, University of South Carolina, 1929) and *South Carolina Baptists, 1670-1805* (Florence, S.C.: Florence Printing Co., 1935).

[61] "Interesting Life Story" and "Lawyer Campaigned on New County Issue."

[62] *N&C*, March 1, 1891 (2nd edition).

[63] Ibid., (1st edition).

[64] Ibid., (2nd edition). This article first appeared in the *Augusta Chronicle*. Telephone conversation, Eugene N. Zeigler Jr. with the editor.

[65] Telephone conversation, Eugene N. Zeigler Jr. with the editor.


## "A SOUTHERN CAMP," *NEW YORK TRIBUNE*, OCTOBER 14, 1876

[1] William J. Whipper (black) and ex-governor Franklin J. Moses Jr. (white) were elected by the General Assembly in December 1875 when Governor Daniel H. Chamberlain was temporarily away from Columbia. His opposition to both was well known and he eventually prevailed. On Whipper, see Edgar, *South Carolina Encyclopedia*, 1019-20. On Moses, see ibid., 647.

[2] Daniel Henry Chamberlain (1835-1907) was born on a farm in West Brookfield, Massachusetts, ninth child in a large family. He was educated at local academies, graduated from Yale, attended Harvard Law School, and in November 1863 became a lieutenant in the 5th Massachusetts Volunteers, a black contingent. He mustered out as a captain in December 1865, and

the following year came to South Carolina to settle the estate of a deceased friend. During this visit, Chamberlain saw an opportunity to grow cotton and repay school debts. In 1867 he represented Berkeley County in the state constitutional convention and the following year became attorney general. Although associated with a corrupt gang, he never was charged with personal dishonesty. See also Edgar, *South Carolina Encyclopedia,* 143-44.

[3] On Richard Laurence Manning (1816-89), see Edgar, *South Carolina Encyclopedia*, 588; on Benjamin Franklin Perry (1805-86), see ibid., 713; on Joseph Brevard Kershaw (1822-1894), see ibid., 516; on Charles H. Simonton (1829-1904), see *Dictionary of American Biography* 17: 174-75.

[4] Major Lewis Merrill of the 7th Cavalry arrived in Yorkville, S.C., in March 1871 to assume control of the cavalry in the state. Richard M. Zuczek, *State of Rebellion: People's War in Reconstruction South Carolina, 1865-1877* (Columbia: University of South Carolina Press, 1996), 94-9.

[5] Early in 1876 Congressman Hill of Georgia delivered an impassioned speech in Congress attacking the notion that the Andersonville prison conditions justified continuing attacks on the South and Southerners. Congressman James G. Blaine of Maine had claimed that Davis and other former confederates still bore responsibility for the "murders" of Andersonville and should not therefore receive amnesty. See Ben Cloyd, *Haunted by Atrocity: Civil War Prisons in American Memory* (Baton Rouge: Louisiana State University Press, 2010). Thanks to Chris Barr of the Andersonville National Historic Site for help with this note.

[6] Alexander Stephens of Georgia, a former member of the U.S. House and vice president of the Confederate States of America, was reelected to Congress in 1873 and served until 1882; John Brown Gordon of Georgia, former Confederate lieutenant general, served in the U.S. Senate from 1873-80 and 1891-97; Lucius Quintus Cincinnatus Lamar represented Mississippi in the U.S. House of Representatives before the Civil War and from 1872 to 1876 before being elected to the U.S. Senate; Benjamin Hill of Georgia won a seat in the U.S. Congress in December 1875, and two years later moved to the U.S. Senate; J. Proctor Knott of Kentucky served in the U.S. House of Representatives from 1863 to 1871 and 1875-83.

[7] On the Mississippi plan, see Budiansky, *Bloody Shirt*, 221-23 and 267-68.

[8] The *Daily Enterprise*, established in 1876, ceased publication that same year. It was the daily edition of the weekly *Enterprise and Mountaineer*.

[9] The Columbia daily was the *Columbia Register*, founded in July 1875.

[10] R. Barnwell Rhett Jr. edited the short-lived *Charleston Journal of Commerce*,

established in the spring of 1876 while Francis Dawson's *News and Courier* still was advocating the reelection of Republican Daniel Chamberlain. On Rhett, see Carl R. Osthaus, *Partisans of the Southern Press: Editorial Spokesmen of the Nineteenth Century* (Lexington: University of Kentucky Press, 1994), 69-94, and William C. Davis, *Rhett: The Turbulent Life and Times of a Fire-Eater* (Columbia: University of South Carolina Press, 1994).

[11] For details of the extravaganza, see the Charleston *News and Courier* (hereafter *N&C*), June 27-29, 1876), which used the opportunity to heap praise upon Governor Chamberlain, one of the principal speakers.

[12] According to "A Cutting Affray," *N&C*, June 29, 1876, the attack was related to "impudence" given by Morgan Alston, "a colored hall-boy at the Charleston Hotel" to "a young Augustan, a member of the Richmond Hussars of Augusta," a year earlier. During the centennial, Alston was sitting on the hotel steps, tumbler in hand, when the Augustan "was induced, by some insolent remark from him, to strike him over the head." Alston "flung the tumbler into the face of the Hussar, who drew his knife and stabbed him twice" in the back.

[13] On the railroads, see Williamson, *After Slavery: the Negro in South Carolina during Reconstruction, 1861-1877*, 384-87, and Reynolds, *Reconstruction in South Carolina*, 174-75, 465-70.

[14] On Matthew Calbraith Butler (1836-1909), Confederate general and U.S. senator (1877-95), see Edgar, *South Carolina Encyclopedia*, 111. On Martin Witherspoon Gary (1831-81), Confederate general and "the most uncompromising leader of the 'Straight-out' faction," see ibid., 361.

[15] This may have been the weekly *Edgefield Monitor*, edited by E. W. McLenna, though most sources say it was founded in 1877.

[16] On the mid-May murder near Abbeville of Mr. and Mrs. John L. Harmon and the lynching of six black men thought to be the assailants, see *N&C*, May 25, 26, 1876, including an editorial in the latter that defends the lynching. The men were shot by at least 100 men in a crowd of at least 500.

[17] On the Hamburg Massacre, see *N&C*, July 10-12, 1876; Budiansky, *Bloody Shirt*, 221-47.

[18] "Glencoe" refers to a massacre that took place on February 13, 1692, in the highlands of Scotland. Thirty-eight members of the Clan MacDonald of Glencoe were killed when soldiers claimed they hadn't quickly enough pledged allegiance to the new monarchs, William and Mary. Forty women and children died of exposure after their homes were burned. "Wyoming" concerns the battle of the Wyoming Valley in Pennsylvania on July 3, 1778,

in which more than 300 Patriots were killed. After the battle, rumors claimed that Iroquois raiders, who served with the Tories, tortured to death 30 to 40 men who had surrendered.

[19] On the proposed duels, see Susan Millar Williams and Stephen G. Hoffius, *Upheaval in Charleston: Earthquake and Murder on the Eve of Jim Crow* (Athens: University of Georgia Press, 2011), 96-7.

[20] "To send to Conventry" means to refuse to associate with. Although the origin is unclear, it perhaps grew out of events associated with England's seventeenth-century revolution.

[21] This confrontation, sparked by an attempt to arrest two blacks charged with robbing the home of a white woman, led to a riotous weekend early in September in which at least five whites and perhaps as many as 100 blacks died. The uproar was quelled by federal troops stationed in Aiken. See Mark M. Smith, "'All Is Not Quiet in Our Hellish County': Facts, Fiction, Politics, and Race—The Ellenton Riot of 1876," *SCHM* 95, no. 2 (April 1994): 143–155.

[22] The *N&C* covered the Ellenton riot September 19-25, 1876. On September 21 the paper ran a long subhead that included, "Two Whites Certainly Killed . . . Only Twenty-five or Thirty Negroes Killed So Far."

[23] In 1678 William Bedloe and Titus Oates claimed to have known about a plot to restore the Catholic religion in England.

[24] Hampton, more than $1 million in debt, declared bankruptcy in 1868. Much of his furniture was auctioned on the courthouse steps in Columbia. Rod Andrew Jr., *Wade Hampton: Confederate Warrior to Southern Redeemer* (Chapel Hill: University of North Carolina, 2008), 315-16. However he still owned Wild Woods plantation in Mississippi, about 835 acres. Walter Brian Cisco, *Wade Hampton: Confederate Warrior, Conservative Statesman* (Washington, D.C.: Brassey's Inc., 2004), 198-99.

## "A SOUTHERN CAMP," *NEW YORK TRIBUNE,* OCTOBER 16, 1876

[1] Townsend is quoting part of the preface to *Corruption and Intolerance* (1808) by Thomas Moore.

[2] On Benjamin Hill of Georgia and J. Proctor Knott of Kentucky, see note 6, page 151.

[3] John C. Calhoun (1782-1850), William Campbell Preston (1794-1860), William Lowndes (1782-1822), George McDuffie (1790-1851), and Robert Y. Hayne (1791-1839).

[4] Before the Civil War, Hamilton Fish (1808-93) was governor of New York

and U.S. senator; he was President Ulysses S. Grant's secretary of state from 1869 until 1877. Samuel J. Tilden, former governor of New York, was the Democratic candidate for president in 1876. Charles Francis Adams (1807-86), grandson of President John Adams and son of President John Quincy Adams, was nominated for the vice presidency in 1848 and 1872. Thomas F. Bayard (1828-98) of Delaware was a U.S. senator and candidate for the Democratic nomination for president.

[5] After a bloody battle in New Orleans in 1874, Lt. Gov. Davidson Penn was briefly named governor with the support of the White League. When the federal government refused to recognize Penn, he backed down.

[6] For a modern study of black support for Hampton, see Edmund L. Drago, *Hurrah for Hampton! Black Red Shirts in South Carolina during Reconstruction* (Fayetteville: University of Arkansas Press, 1998).

[7] "*Vi et armis*": by force of arms.

[8] On the Charleston riot, see *N&C*, September 7, 8, 1876, and Melinda Meek Hennessey, "Racial Violence during Reconstruction: The 1876 Riots in Charleston and Cainhoy," *SCHM* 86, no. 2 (April 1985): 104–05.

[9] In Vicksburg, Mississippi, in the summer of 1874, "the city's white residents organized a People's or White Man's party. At the August municipal election, it patrolled the streets in armed gangs and succeeded in intimidating enough black voters to oust the city's Republic officeholders." Eric Foner, *Reconstruction: America's Unfinished Revolution, 1863-1877* (New York: Harper & Row, 1988), 558.

## "THE POLITICAL CONDITION OF SOUTH CAROLINA," *THE ATLANTIC MONTHLY* 39, NO. 232 (FEBRUARY 1877)

[1] In the 1868 election Robert K. Scott won about 75 percent of the votes for governor. Lemuel Boozer was elected lieutenant governor, Daniel Chamberlain was attorney general, Niles G. Parker was treasurer, Francis L. Cardozo was secretary of state, and Franklin J. Moses Jr. was speaker of the house.

[2] On the railroads, see note 13, page 152. On the State House renovations, see Reynolds, *Reconstruction in South Carolina*, 476-82. On the public printing bills, see Reynolds, *Reconstruction in South Carolina*, 473-76, and Williamson, *After Slavery*, 388.

[3] On taxes, see Reynolds, *Reconstruction in South Carolina*, 134, 160, 170, and 240-42.

[4] On the Land Commission, see Williamson, *After Slavery*, 142-48, and

Reynolds, *Reconstruction in South Carolina*, 118-19, and 135.

⁵ This trio consisted of A. J. Willard, Franklin J. Moses Sr., and Jonathan Jasper Wright. Willard, a well-trained New York lawyer, served from 1868 to 1880, the last three years as chief justice. See Ulysses R. Brooks, *South Carolina Bench and Bar* (Columbia: State Co., 1908), 36-9. Moses, a Sumter native and father of the man who headed up a thoroughly corrupt state administration (1872-74), was associate justice from 1865 to 1868 and then chief justice until his death in 1877. See *Dictionary of American Biography* (New York: Charles Scribner's Sons, 1920- ), 13: 275-76. Wright, an able legal mind from Pennsylvania and said to have been the state's first black lawyer, was on the high court from 1870 to 1877. See Edgar, *South Carolina Encyclopedia*, 1050-51. The judicial careers of all three, but especially Wright, are discussed in J. Clay Smith, "The Reconstruction of Justice Jonathan Jasper Wright," in *At Freedom's Door: African American Founding Fathers and Lawyers in Reconstruction South Carolina*, ed. James Lowell Underwood and W. Lewis Burke Jr. (Columbia: University of South Carolina Press, 2000), 72-89.

⁶ On the pardons, see Reynolds, *Reconstruction in South Carolina*, 135.

⁷ Horatio Seymour, former governor of New York, and Francis Preston Blair Jr., former Union general, were the Democratic candidates for president and vice president in 1868.

⁸ This gentleman was Vermont native Richard B. Carpenter, who came to South Carolina from Kentucky and served as judge of the first judicial circuit (Charleston and Orangeburg counties) from 1868 to 1870. See Brooks, *South Carolina Bench and Bar,* 167-68.

⁹ Horace Greeley, editor of the *New York Tribune*, was the Democratic candidate for president in 1872.

¹⁰ On Daniel H. Chamberlain, see note 2, pages 150-51.

¹¹ On William J. Whipper and Franklin J. Moses Jr., see note 1, page 150.

¹² On the centennial, see the *N&C*, June 27-29, 1876.

¹³ Samuel J. Tilden, the Democratic candidate for president, received a majority of the popular vote, but lost the Electoral College vote to Republican Rutherford B. Hayes.

¹⁴ Actually, some of these events occurred before the Fort Moultrie celebration. Alfred Rush, a member of the lower house from Darlington, was shot from ambush while returning from a church picnic in mid-May. *N&C*, May 15, 1876. Within two weeks, six blacks were lynched in Edgefield County following the brutal murder of an elderly white couple. *N&C*, May

25, 26, 1876. Earlier in the same year, according to the *Marion Star*, January 19, sixteen men were arrested for lynching Archie Matheson in Marlboro County. Matheson (black) allegedly assaulted Mrs. Angus McDonald (white), a resident of the Clio area, on January 1. All of those arraigned, including Mrs. McDonald's husband, soon were set free. The circumstances of the second Marlboro lynching mentioned by Townsend are not known. On the Hamburg Massacre, see note 17, page 152.

[15] Joachim Murat (1767-1815) was the brilliant cavalry leader who Napoleon made king of Naples in 1808.

[16] On the Mississippi plan, see note 7, page 151.

[17] Robert Augustus Toombs was a Georgia congressman who helped draft the Compromise of 1850, and was elevated to the U.S. Senate. Benjamin Harvey Hill, Georgia statesman and Confederate senator, was a rival of Toombs who defended Jefferson Davis's Confederate administration. John Brown Gordon, another Georgia political figure, was in command of a wing of Lee's army at Appomattox. For more on each of these men, see "The New Georgia Encyclopedia" (http://www.georgiaencyclopedia.org) (accessed July 14, 2012).

[18] On the Ellenton riot, see note 21, page 153.

[19] In October 1876 President Ulysses S. Grant ordered all available forces in the Division of the Atlantic, about 1,150 officers and men, to report to Columbia. Zuczek, *State of Rebellion*, 177-79.

[20] On the Charleston riot of September 6-7, 1876, see note 8, page 154.

[21] Both factions agreed to go unarmed to a political meeting held on October 16 at Cainhoy in Charleston County. They failed to keep their promises. When shooting started, whites found themselves at the mercy of blacks. See Hennessey, "Racial Violence during Reconstruction," 107–09, and Elise Pinckney, "The Cainhoy Riot as Remembered by Jim Alston," *SCHM* 86, no. 2 (April 1985): 158–60.

[22] In 1874 Democrats won a "tidal wave" of races in the North, including Massachusetts, New Hampshire, New Jersey, Pennsylvania, Illinois, and Ohio, as well as Indiana. Foner, *Reconstruction*, 523.

[23] By "repeating," Townsend means voting more than once.

[24] While campaigning for lieutenant governor in 1900, Senator Ben Tillman's nephew James H. Tillman boasted that he voted in Edgefield County in 1876, though he had been born just seven years before.

[25] Franklin J. Moses Jr. (1838-1906), private secretary to Governor Francis W. Pickens and one of the men who raised the Confederate flag over Fort

Sumter in April 1861, became a Radical Republican in 1867. As governor (1872-74) he presided over a venal administration. Some Sumter relatives were so chagrined they changed their names to "Harby" or "DeLeon." On Moses, see *DAB* 13:275-76; Benjamin Ginsberg, *Moses of South Carolina: A Jewish Scalawag during Radical Reconstruction* (Baltimore, Md.: Johns Hopkins University Press, 2010), 191 (name change).

[26] Ex-Confederates Davidson B. Penn and Louis Alfred Wiltz were involved in unsuccessful attempts to oust Louisiana's carpetbag governor William Pitt Kellogg in 1874-75.

[27] Virginia journalist and author Edward W. Pollard (1831-72) churned out a steady stream of articles and books, all bitterly prejudiced in favor of his beloved South. Alexander Stephens, former vice-president of the Confederacy, was doing much the same, as was Admiral Raphael Semmes, one-time commander of the raider *Alabama*.

[28] *Nolens volens*: unwillingly.

[29] A reference to the use of native troops by the East India Company, "sepoy" being the English spelling of "sipahi" (Persian and Urdu word for soldier).

[30] Charles Nordoff, Prussian-born journalist and Washington correspondent of the *Herald* in the 1870s, was author of *The Freedmen of South Carolina* (1863) and *The Cotton States in the Spring and Summer of 1875* (1876). In the latter work (p. 15), he predicted a Whig revival in some parts of the South.

[31] Some such claims were paid in the 1870s to Southerners who could prove loyalty to the Union throughout the war. See John Hammond Moore, "Getting Uncle Sam's Dollars: South Carolinians and the Southern Claims Commission, 1871-1880," *SCHM* 82 (July 1981): 248-62.

[32] In 1873 Spain seized the *Virginius* on the high seas, a vessel belonging to a Cuban revolutionary group based in New York, and shot fifty-three American and British citizens as filibusterers. In the end, Spain apologized and paid indemnities.

[33] The two Republican leaders probably were Christopher Columbus Bowen and Edmund W. McGregor Mackey. On Bowen, see Hyman Rubin III, *South Carolina Scalawags* (Columbia: University of South Carolina Press, 2006) and, in a scornful obituary, *N&C*, June 24, 1880. On Mackey, see http://bioguide.congress.gov/scripts/biodisplay.pl?index=M000024 (accessed February 13, 2013).

[34] Thomas Holt found that of the 123 members of the South Carolina house of representatives, 1875-76, 89 were Republicans and 34 Democrats; 71 of the Republicans were African Americans. Thomas Holt, *Black over White:*

*Negro Political Leadership in South Carolina during Reconstruction* (Urbana: University of Illinois Press, 1977, 75-6.

[35] *Nem con* (*nemine contradicente*): no one contradicting, unanimously.

## "SOUTH CAROLINA MORALS,"
### *THE ATLANTIC MONTHLY* 39, NO. 234 (APRIL 1877)

[1] Townsend is referring to the views of Percy Greg, a prolific British essayist who disliked modern times and yearned for the age of feudalism. One of his earliest works, *The Verge of Night*, appeared in 1875 and was followed in 1880 by *Across the Zodiac*, a foundation stone of twentieth-century science fiction.

[2] According to Herodotus's *History of the Persian Wars* (Book IV) (440 B.C.), the Scythians, upon their return from Media, c.572 B.C., faced a slave rebellion. They were unsuccessful until one of their leaders suggested they change tactics: "So long as they see us with arms in our hands, they imagine themselves our equals in birth and bravery; but let them behold us with no other weapon but the whip, and they will feel that they are our slaves, and flee before us." Herodotus says the slaves were so astounded that they forgot to fight and ran away.

[3] Maryland's Reverdy Johnson, a distinguished constitutional lawyer, served as U.S. senator in the 1840s and again in the 1860s, was attorney general in the Zachary Taylor cabinet, and worked hard to keep his state in the Union. As minister to Great Britain (1868-69), his policy toward the South during Reconstruction was both unclear and inconsistent.

[4] William Lloyd Garrison, a native of Massachusetts, co-edited the Baltimore newspaper *Quaker Genius of Universal Emancipation* until he was convicted of libel for claiming that a shipper was involved in the slave trade. After spending seven weeks in prison, in 1831 he returned to New England.

[5] Helots were state-owned serfs of ancient Sparta who, although sometimes used in wartime as soldiers, experienced extremely harsh treatment. Their rulers, constantly in fear of an insurrection, permitted an annual slaughter of their ranks and maintained a secret force designed to eliminate potential troublemakers.

[6] This duel, which occurred during the Nullification crisis of 1832-1833, pitted Greenville editor Benjamin Perry of the *Mountaineer* against Turner Bynum of the newly founded *Southern Sentinel*. Convinced that Bynum was determined to ruin him and his Unionist cause, Perry responded to a furious blast with a challenge. In the encounter, much to Perry's regret, Bynum was mortally wounded. See Adele Kibler, *Benjamin F. Perry, South Carolina*

*Unionist* (Durham, N.C.: Duke University Press, 1946), 124-34.

[7] *Ex gratia*: as a favor.

[8] This probably refers to Benjamin Franklin Whittemore, who helped found the *New Era* in Darlington in July 1865.

[9] Squire Weston, neighbor of Thomas Alworthy and father of Sophia in Henry Fielding's *The History of Tom Jones* (1749), insisted his daughter marry money.

## "SOUTH CAROLINA SOCIETY,"
## *THE ATLANTIC MONTHLY 39*, NO. 236 (JUNE 1877)

[1] George Bancroft, *History of the United States from the Discovery of the American Continent* (Boston: Little Brown, 1859, 17th edition), II: 170-71.

[2] Chevalier was sent to the United States in 1834 under government patronage to inspect public works. These lines are from "Letter X" in which Chevalier actually was comparing Virginians and Yankees, not Southerners per se. See his *Society, Manners and Politics in the United States: Being a Series of Letters on North America* (Boston: Weeks, Jordan and Co., 1839), 114-15.

[3] Matthew C. Butler played a central role in the Hamburg Massacre of July 1876. He served as U.S. senator from 1877 until 1895. Edgar, *South Carolina Encyclopedia*, 111. The "kitchen organ" referred to was the *Daily Union-Herald* (published as the *Union-Herald*, 1876-77). It was created in May 1873 by merger of the *Columbia Daily Union* and *Daily Evening Herald*. Among those associated with the paper were T. C. Andrews and J. G. Thompson.

[4] On R. Barnwell Rhett Jr., see note 10, pages 151-52, first essay. Henry Adams once said Rhett was the type of Southerner from whom "one could learn nothing but bad temper, bad manners, poker, and treason." Adams, *The Education of Henry Adams* (1907). Pelham helped found the *Columbia Register* in July 1875. William C. Preston headed up South Carolina College, 1845-51; Robert W. Barnwell did so 1835-41 and 1866-73.

[5] In a diary now at the South Caroliniana Library, Grace Brown Elmore described how, in May 1865, she told ex-slaves of her Columbia household she could no longer pay them and they were free to leave. All promised to stay, but then simply disappeared. On June 25 she wrote, "I don't like to live among pots and kettles." See her diary, 1860-1866, which is slightly different from the published volume edited by Marli Frances Weiner, *A Heritage of Woe: The Civil War Diary of Grace Brown Elmore, 1861-1868* (Athens: University of Georgia Press, 1997).

[6] Not entirely. A Columbia-area matron who owned more than 200 slaves noted on April 4, 1861, after a conversation with a little black girl, "I did not know how my negroes hated white folks & how they talked about me." See John Hammond Moore, ed., *A Plantation Mistress on the Eve of the Civil War: The Diary of Keziah Goodwyn Hopkins Brevard* (Columbia: University of South Carolina Press, 1993), 111.

[7] Actually, it is not clear that Geoffrey and Toinette, leading figures in a work by Albion Winegar Tourgée, ever became husband and wife. First published in 1874 as *Toinette: A Novel*, with Henry Churton (pseudonym) as author, this tale of miscegenation reappeared in 1875 and 1879 with minor title changes and then in 1881 as *The Royal Gentleman* with a completely different conclusion. In the latter, the lovers, once master and slave and burdened by the effects of that relationship, definitely parted.

[8] Johann Heinrich Pestalozzi, Swiss educational reformer, is best known for *Leonard and Gertrude* (1781), which tells how a good and devoted woman reformed her household and then an entire village. His German successor, Friedrich Wilhelm August Froebel (1782-1852), father of the kindergarten, and English philosopher Herbert Spencer (1820-1903) expressed well the general formula of progress that pervaded late-nineteenth-century thought.

[9] "Rozinante": Don Quixote's steed.

[10] These are popular journals of the 1870s.

[11] On March 1, 1878, the General Assembly ended public executions; instead, they were to take place within an enclosure in the presence of county officials, the state solicitor, attorneys, relatives, and not more than ten other individuals as witnesses. *Acts and Joint Resolutions of the General Assembly of the State of South Carolina . . . 1875-76* (Columbia: Republican Printing Co., 1876), Act #362, p. 381.

[12] British poet William Collins composed this ode in 1746.

[13] Visits of English writer Harriet Martineau (1802-76) in 1834 produced *Society in America* (1837), *A Retrospect of Western Travel* (1838), and various articles that brought the abolition struggle to the attention of the British public. On the Calhoun Monument in Charleston, dedicated in 1887, see Thomas J. Brown, "The Monumental Legacy of Calhoun," in *The Memory of the Civil War in American Culture*, eds. Alice Fahs and Joan Waugh (Chapel Hill: University of North Carolina Press, 2004), 130–56.

[14] Nonetheless, the socially important Brown Fellowship Society in Charleston limited its membership to individuals of mixed race. Edgar, *South Carolina Encyclopedia*, 104.

## "THE RESULT IN SOUTH CAROLINA,"
### *THE ATLANTIC MONTHLY* 41, NO. 243 (JANUARY 1878)

[1] In a footnote, Townsend writes, "A thousand buildings, including a dozen towns or portions of towns, worth a million dollars, were burnt by incendiaries within the year preceding last April."

[2] "The senate," Townsend adds in a footnote, "resolved to meet the republican house to elect a United States senator by joint ballot, and the republican senators, and consequently the majority, actually did so. Mr. Corbin was thus elected. But the democratic senators, though a minority, met in joint session with the democratic house, and elected General Butler." David T. Corbin, Dartmouth graduate and a shrewd lawyer from Vermont, came to South Carolina with the Freedmen's Bureau in 1865 and served in the state senate from 1868 to 1872 when he became an anti-Moses reformer. Considered a fair man of good repute, although not free of controversy, Corbin never took his seat in the U.S. Senate; however, he remained active in local politics until moving to Illinois in 1886. See N. Louise Bailey, Mary L. Morgan, and Carolyn R. Taylor, *Biographical Directory of the South Carolina Senate, 1776-1985* (Columbia: University of South Carolina Press, 1986), 1: 199.

[3] "Patent outside" refers to mass-produced, four-page newspapers—pages one and four printed by some syndicate, pages two and three left blank to be filled with local news and regional ads.

[4] "Gibing": shifting around, changing course. It may be a variation of the nautical term "jibe."

[5] Jonathan Jasper Wright resigned from the Supreme Court in August 1877. See note 5, p. 155.

[6] A. J. Willard served as chief justice from 1877 to 1880. See note 5, p. 155.

[7] Many of these black Republican officeholders are identified in Eric Foner, *Freedom's Lawmakers: A Directory of Black Officeholders during Reconstruction*. Rev. ed. (Baton Rouge: Louisiana State University Press, 1996).

[8] It is often said that members of this powerful European dynasty, ousted by Napoleon I, forgot nothing and learned nothing during their years in exile.

[9] Townsend added in a footnote, "I have seen this comparison used by Southern papers so often that I am almost ashamed to repeat it."

[10] According to the *New York Times*, August 17, 1877, Postmaster-General David M. Key, Tennessee politician and Confederate veteran, spoke briefly in Vermont at ceremonies marking the centennial of the Battle of Bennington. Traveling with President Rutherford B. Hayes, Key said he took the warmth of

greeting not as a personal compliment, but "an indication of fraternal feeling on the part of our Northern friends for their erring Southern brethren." The South was furious. The *N&C*, August 18, 1877, retorted, "Erring be hanged! Southerners are not willing to be brethren of any living people on such terms. They do not admit that they erred. They did not err. They believed they were right. They were right."

[11] An obvious reference to the 13th, 14th, and 15th amendments outlawing slavery and protecting civil rights.

[12] However, late in April 1878 the *Azor* left Charleston with 274 blacks bound for Liberia. Journalist Alfred B. Williams accompanied the group and described the voyage and reception in the *News and Courier*, material later published as a ten-chapter pamphlet. See Alfred B. Williams, *The Liberian Exodus: An Account of Voyage of the First Emigrants in the Bark "Azor" and their Reception* (Charleston: News and Courier Book Presses, 1878); George B. Tindall, "The Liberian Exodus of 1878," *SCHM* 53 (July 1952): 133-45.

[13] Townsend appended this footnote: "Indeed, so many promises were made to the colored democrats during the canvass that a few dozen of them have unavoidably been made justices, constables, etc.; a half dozen have been appointed to really high positions; while in Charleston County, *mirabile dictu*, three subservient colored men were elected, on the democratic ticket, to the legislature."

[14] The South Carolina College, now the University of South Carolina, was closed in 1877 "to purge it of the Republican influences that [white leadership led by Governor Wade Hampton] believed had sullied it." The school reopened in 1880. The only state-run college with an African American student majority was founded in 1896 as the Colored Normal, Industrial, Agricultural and Mechanical College of South Carolina. It is now South Carolina State University. Edgar, *South Carolina Encyclopedia*, 991-92.

### "WILD WITH ALL REGRET: A TALE OF RECONSTRUCTION"

[1] Townsend appended twenty-one footnotes to his poems. All for "Wild with All Regret" are reproduced in original or expanded form. The first one told readers that counties were known as "districts" in South Carolina until 1868, the area ruled by a district court.

[2] "The Oaks" was a well-known Middleton plantation near Goose Creek in Berkeley County noted for its elegant avenue of live oaks. The mansion burned in 1840.

[3] Whitmire appears to be a composite of Benjamin Franklin Whittemore

(1824-1894), carpetbag state senator from Darlington County, Joe Crews of Laurens County (a former slave trader killed from ambush in 1875), and various other Republican Radicals. In October 1873 Whittemore purchased Ashley Hall near Charleston, longtime seat of the Bull family, at a sheriff's sale. However, there was no grand mansion, the structure having been burned by Yankee troops in 1865. (According to the chronology sketched by Townsend, Whitmire's purchase of "The Oaks" took place in the late 1860s.) For a brief history of Ashley Hall, see Henry DeSaussure Bull, "Ashley Hall Plantation," *SCHM* 53 (April 1952): 61-6.

[4] Townsend notes that "the first Monday in every month is known as 'Sales Day' in South Carolina, being set aside by law as the time on which all judicial sales must be made at the Court House door of each County by the Sheriff and other officers. On Sales Days thousands of people, white and black, throng in on foot or horseback, or in buggies, to the County towns, to sell produce, cotton, eggs, chickens, &c., swap horses or buggies, buy goods, talk to the lawyers and merchants, to drink and fight."

[5] Emory Upton (1839-81), a famous Union officer of the Civil War, was a strict disciplinarian who drilled men in all kinds of weather. An expert on tactics, he committed suicide a few months before his forty-second birthday.

[6] These words may have been addressed to Townsend's father.

[7] Allie, of course, represents South Carolina during Reconstruction.

[8] Salvator Rosa (1615-73), Italian poet and painter.

[9] In a brief footnote, Townsend points the reader to Macaulay's *Milton* and a tale by Ludovico Ariosto (1474-1533) of a fairy who, during certain seasons, appeared in the form of a snake.

[10] Townsend again refers the reader to Macaulay's *Milton*. See Charles Wallace French, ed., *Macaulay's Essays on Milton and Addison* (London, 1902), 32-34.

[11] "Titmouse" may refer to a small, petty, or insignificant individual.

[12] Townsend notes these comments are inspired by lines found in William Wordsworth's "Rob Roy's Grave" (1807): "That they should take, who have the power, and they should keep who can." This sequence obviously refers to themes present in naturalist Charles Darwin's *Origin of the Species* (1852) and Spencer's system of unified science expressed in *First Principles* (1862).

[13] The source of this digression—"Offitt the Bread Winner"—is not known.

[14] This apparently is "poetic license" at work. No such motion is printed in the *Senate Journal* of the late 1860s, the period when Townsend indicates these events occurred.

[15] Knout is a type of whip used to flog criminals. Townsend has in mind

Alexander II (1818-81), who was killed by a terrorist bomb on March 1, 1881.

[16] Gessler was the tyrannical Austrian bailiff who forced William Tell to shoot an apple from his son's head. Brutus, of course, killed Caesar.

[17] Wade Hampton's Red Shirts of 1876.

[18] Confederate veteran George Washington Cable (1844-1925) was a New Orleans journalist and writer who became an early advocate of freedmen's rights. As a social reformer, he also spoke out for abolition of convict labor and changes in elections laws and prison administration.

[19] John Howard (1726-1790) was an influential prison reformer and author of *The State of the Prisons in England and Wales* (1777). In a footnote, Townsend, who appears to have shared Howard's concern, calls attention to a grand jury presentment featured in the *News and Courier*, February 29, 1884, critical of the Charleston County Jail. In addition to recommending fixed salaries, not fees, for county officers, jurors said the jail was mismanaged, had neither rules nor routine, needed many repairs and a better kitchen, and was using well water, not city water. Filthy cesspools were evident, they said, and prisoners, too many of them awaiting trial, were roaming about aimlessly.

[20] These words were inspired, Townsend observes, by lines in Henry Timrod's poem "Charleston": "And maidens, with such eyes as would grow dim over a bleeding hound."

# Bibliography

Andrew, Rod, Jr. *Wade Hampton: Confederate Warrior to Southern Redeemer.* Chapel Hill: University of North Carolina, 2008.

Brooks, U. R. *South Carolina Bench and Bar.* Columbia, S.C.: The State Co., 1908.

Budianski, Stephen. *The Bloody Shirt: Terror After Appomattox.* New York: Viking, 2008.

Davis, William C. *Rhett: The Turbulent Life and Times of a Fire-Eater.* Columbia: University of South Carolina Press, 1994.

Edgar, Walter. *South Carolina Encyclopedia.* Columbia: University of South Carolina Press, 2006.

Drago, Edmund L. *Hurrah for Hampton! Black Red Shirts in South Carolina during Reconstruction.* Fayetteville: University of Arkansas Press, 1998.

Foner, Eric. *Freedom's Lawmakers: A Directory of Black Officeholders during Reconstruction.* Rev. ed. Baton Rouge: Louisiana State University Press, 1996.

—. *Reconstruction: America's Unfinished Revolution, 1863-1877.* New York: Harper and Row, 1988.

Hennessey, Melinda Meek. "Racial Violence during Reconstruction: The 1876 Riots in Charleston and Cainhoy," *South Carolina Historical Magazine* 86 (April 1985): 100–12.

Holt, Thomas. *Black over White: Negro Political Leadership in South Carolina during Reconstruction.* Urbana: University of Illinois Press, 1977.

King, G. Wayne. *Rise up So Early: A History of Florence County, South Carolina.* Spartanburg, S.C.: Published for the Florence County Historical Commission by the Reprint Co., 1981.

Pinckney, Elise. "The Cainhoy Riot as Remembered by Jim Alston," *South Carolina Historical Magazine* 86 (July 1985): 158–60.

Reynolds, John S. *Reconstruction in South Carolina, 1865-1877.* Columbia, S.C.: The State Co., 1905.

Smith, Mark M. "'All Is Not Quiet in Our Hellish County': Facts, Fiction, Politics, and Race—The Ellenton Riot of 1876," *South Carolina Historical Magazine* 95 (April 1994): 142–55.

Zeigler, Eugene N., Jr. *Village to City: Florence, South Carolina, 1853-1893.* Spartanburg, S.C.: The Reprint Co., 2008.

Zuczek, Richard M. *State of Rebellion: People's War in Reconstruction South Carolina, 1865-1877* (Columbia: University of South Carolina Press, 1996).

# Acknowledgments

This story could not have been told without the cooperation and assistance of Belton O'Neall Townsend's grandson, Eugene N. Zeigler, and his great-grandson, Benjamin T. Zeigler. In addition I'd like to thank the Darlington County Historical Commission, the James A. Rogers Library at Francis Marion University, the South Caroliniana Library at the University of South Carolina (especially Allen Stokes), and Patrick G. Scott, professor of English at the University of South Carolina.

My very special thanks go to Debbie Bloom, manager of the Walker Local & Family History Center at the Richland Library in Columbia, S.C., for her in-depth review of Townsend material lodged in various depositories in Darlington and Florence counties. Without her help these pages would not be before your eyes.

Tracing the career of an anonymous writer whose work has gained front-page status presents special problems, especially when that individual is associated with Mark Twain and Henry Wadsworth Longfellow. Needless to add, it has been an uphill fight, but I believe well worth it.

A portion of the introduction was published earlier as "Triumph and Tragedy: The Short Life of Belton O'Neall Townsend" in the *South Carolina Review* 38 (Fall 2005), 41-52.

# Index

The abbreviation BOT stands for Belton O'Neall Townsend.

# About the Author

Born on his family's farm in Houlton, Maine, in October 1924, John Hammond Moore helped pick potatoes, cared for crops and livestock, and was educated in local schools. He attended the University of Maine for one year and then volunteered for wartime duty in the United States Navy. Trained as a quartermaster, he joined the crew of the *LSM-R 193*, a pioneer rocket ship constructed in Charleston, South Carolina, which took part in the Okinawa campaign in April 1945

With peace, Moore enrolled in Hamilton College in Clinton, N.Y., where he received his AB degree in June 1949. Three months later he joined the staff of the *Daily Commercial* in Bangor, Maine. In the fall of 1950 he began graduate study in American history at the University of Virginia, earning an MA in 1953 and a PhD in 1961. During these years he was also a reporter for the weekly *Virginia Gazette* in Williamsburg, Virginia, and served on the staff of the McGraw-Hill Book Company in New York City as a salesman and writer.

His teaching career included consecutive three-year stints at Winthrop College in Rock Hill, South Carolina, Georgia State University in Atlanta, and Macquairie University in Sydney, Australia. These contacts led to research in various aspects of regional history as well as the tale of German and Italian POWs in America during World War II. Upon his return to the States from Australia, he lived for several years in Washington, D.C., and then moved to Columbia, South Carolina, where he continues his research and publication efforts. He is the author of eighteen books and editor of five more.